BRIDGE OF THE WORLD

BRIDGE OF THE WORLD

ROBERTO HARRISON

LITMUS PRESS | 2017

ISBN: 978-1-933959-33-7
Cover artwork by Laura Tack from the Decay series: *Decay 1* (front), *Decay 4* (back)
Design and typesetting by HR Hegnauer

Litmus Press is a program of Ether Sea Projects, Inc., a 501(c)(3) non-profit literature and arts organization. Dedicated to supporting innovative, cross-genre writing, the press publishes the work of translators, poets, and other writers, and organizes public events in their support. We encourage interaction between poets and visual artists by featuring contemporary artworks on the covers of our books. By actualizing the potential linguistic, cultural, and political benefits of international literary exchange, we aim to ensure that our poetic communities remain open-minded and vital.

Litmus Press publications are made possible by the New York State Council on the Arts with support from Governor Andrew Cuomo and the New York State Legislature. Additional support for Litmus Press comes from the Leslie Scalapino – O Books Fund, individual members and donors. All contributions are fully tax-deductible.

Cataloging-in-publication data is available from the Library of Congress.

Litmus Press   Small Press Distribution
925 Bergen Street, Suite 405   1341 Seventh Street
Brooklyn, New York 11238   Berkeley, California 94710
litmuspress.org   spdbooks.org

for Brenda
as we bridge

RED AND BLACK
CLUSTER OF BEINGS

…in the end, poetry will unify everything.
JOSÉ LEZAMA LIMA

*States of consciousness there are in which Death
is only a change in immortal Life, pain a violent
backwash of the waters of universal delight, limitation
a turning of the Infinite upon itself, evil a circling
of the good around its own perfection; and this
not in abstract conception only, but in actual vision
and in constant and substantial experience.*

SRI AUROBINDO

New Moon for Ecology

I walked a thousand miles
in the event
of Apocalypse, barefoot, and there
I found the horses
to learn to breathe from. Deer
reveal their wilderness
to us as we wander, as we remove
the tires that brought us here, the vacuous
exception of dreams, the dreamless
attention, the dream that holds all of us
to the conflict that one sees, in the heat
and in the snow, the conflict of the dream
that opens its own eyes, sobbing, at the small
darkness that will not comfort
all of me
as I disappear
it will not believe without planes
to be there, without the untold
overabundance of meaning
of a chatter of a throng of bees, the bees
that remember for us
where the flowers are, in this time
of fires and weapons, the deathless
becomes as close to execution
as the careless wind does not remove
the tree that settles through

an arrival and departure, to the sound
of turmoil and the awful sensory
panoramas
that know no country, no escape
to the memories as they surface here
again and become, like the sand, like the wilderness
emptied of its animals, which will return
through the light of the bridge
though not as we can care for them
again. Even the firing squad, the many headed
beast of underlings, the serpent revealed
to be my soul, in this mythos
which is not a story. in this mythos which
was based on fear (but became something
of love), the collapse
of misunderstanding there
as a child I was to face
an evil of the world
from everywhere at once
with no breathing room,
and it came from me. in the cancer
that will not subside. to reveal the deer
the skin that I wear, the black deer
as I am known to the cellar
in the poverty of light
of the people frequently diminished
by simple signs. those constellations
have no meaning for me, that family

is a set of pebbles
on the ground, and I love them
as I love the earth, but not more. you can see
the head of the lamb
arrive with me, to the Eastern shore
where the horseshoe crabs
eternally
deliver the devil mask
since the beginning of time. I wear it now
to step out of this world, and to see it
in my sleep, which will fill the soil
with the voices of
who is drawn to evil, and who will merely
learn from it. this. there is no end
to the consciousness of abandonment,
inside or out, as it extends
further than the Windows registries
enough so that we can continue to imagine
past the collapse
of the Sun. wars are fought for it, this
occlusion, which is peace, wars
are fought for it because we confuse
ourselves with the smallest node
of the client. wars will come of it because
we have not seen clearly
that only a small continent
a fraction of the network's blood
has been experienced by us, in this world

of absolute and constant assault
of the silhouettes. Silence reveals
the vast rents,
and unknowable vistas that enrich us, but we have
no words
and no ears for these. the inside
was duplicated
long ago, due to a rigidness
which confuses the sacred
and the healing songs
with weakness and material
for the first rose of winter. I sang these songs
and I saw these sacred things
as my mind was dispersed
throughout the endless knots
of hearts in the rise of a network agora
and fully seeing. but now, I've died
through the uncountable, and I arrive
to a place where these things and these
songs, though still protected, become
the light and the dark
that I put together
with the Yoga of Panamá, to carry me
there, as the first and last
Panamanian. And there are uncountably
many of us, evenly spread
across the universe, of every color,
every persuasion, every shape, speaking

every language, of fire or of water, endlessly
propagating to help us. I am here to help
and I am here to die again, to free myself
from all of you
with loving kindness
and compassion, as the Sun promises
to be here tomorrow, or not. as the Moon
reveals itself to be
a new encircled Sunrise

¿Quieres Ser Amigos?

let fly what will fly
let it come down like a storm
of fearful Rinpoches. what language
remains at the end
of my migration, by plane
alone
as an infant, back to Panamá, to forget
always — what were the tears
that brought back the sloth, the coconuts
flown to impoverish
each conversation
from the end of time, as now? no towel
there, but what I searched for, a combination
in the ceiling marked by dots, I tried
to gain entry into heaven, but did not. Angels
have bargained for me, that the Sea
will not replace her own animals
with the ones I've meant to bring, from the light
to arrive with the impoverished,
always sent
to negotiate troubles
in the Canal
by phone and through digital voicing, far away
it began, with *cocuyitos*, a plain effort

Nature to mimic us now. Computers
will gradually disappear, but their light remains,
now that our networks
take on the work of survival, the flash
entered into a slave machine, a caste system
wades into water
and saves itself
from annihilation,
with annihilation
from the salt
that their frozen trauma, like mine, will sever
in its projectiles, the force field increases
with a shelter
that is destroyed, the hiding place
from future heat and salvation. remember that One
serves to reveal the shattered image of true
self knowledge, the instantaneous errors
of friendship
that the Moon ails
to arrive at this, this tearing off of skin
that will remain with the promises, the ritual
entry of flags and prayers
that the nest of snakes
reveals to be One. there is no real survival value
to practices, no real insight into the heart
of the universe, except that in blindness
I see with the troubles that a single soul
might make, a soul to be one in two, to eliminate

the entrances and exits
from the sphere of networks
which includes
the entire universe. Some stopped writing
because they had written their dreams so well. I cannot
stop, because I am just beginning to dream, just
beginning to see
through myself in the world, not
so that I can become
invisible to you
again, but to write invisibly
through my heart, the residence of my mind,
evenly distributed
throughout endless Imagination's
Oceans.

I write the release
of a night sky, because my reptilian
anchor, the frozen tundra of my traumas
will break off as ice floes, as the earth does now,
and we will be one together, to remake the poles,
to place them elsewhere, to find a new constellation
that travels with us through the end
of monuments and compassion. And it's our own fault
for not believing in the power of the wilderness,
in the power of the ancients (of the Imagination's
Seas),

in the events of a bridge
which serves solely to manifest
as a Fourth Form — Panamá. Its two Yogas,
of the earth and of the waters, between the Sea
and the Ocean, its many fishes
that claim us
to fly as butterflies
and remember that the Apostle Islands
claim the capital of the Ojibwa here, in their
residence, where the ashes of my past
pass through, into the lake
of the Pioneers, and back to Panamá. Cry again
for you shall see
how the moments have split
inside, to deliver us
from the possible life
of the extremes of the most noble exhaustion.
Don't tell me again that there's a hierarchy
from which we cannot remove ourselves. I've seen it,
that breathing will bring it all together, as I cannot
breathe, I cannot breathe, and I do not See. Kindness
is the main objective.

A Wreck of Salvation

a sunrise pierces
an edge of the iron

crowd

it counts down
to believe no action

in the unformed

a retreat
has opened.

Silent winter

long

cuts through memory

extricating
a tongue
to find circles

and the country of
water's
seal, keep it

and speak again

through the floor
of an arriving

galaxy

to seal
that sight
is clear

●

resource

●

letter

Man of Sorrows

where does it stop? all because
of a thousand demonic giants
and my attachment to them
will not let them go
'til now
fused to the memory of my fence
which no longer protects
or savages each animal in my winter
link. I am angry at the planets
that have shrunken into the empty
husk of a long dead dog
in the desert, there, remorsefully connected
to the abolished, to the sound of a small
refuge in a world of controls —
accident, new moon for the torturers
one more event on the horizon
of my misunderstood
monster, the reward of a plan of action
that erases you, and makes you tremble
like the mind
that I have not yet gained,
forever. not everyone else
has a ground they built under them
with homes and playgrounds
with a television that does not threaten them
with a remorseless politics

but the few, the proud, the rewarded

for being in a single place

their entire lives. No. that's what love is to you, (No)

a piece of ground that you've worn so thoroughly

that you feel as if

you are a part of the earth. but

I am that earth, not you. I am that Sun, not you.

I am that Moon

that falls on the roof of your house

to destroy the trees

and your antennae, to destroy

the medicines

you think will gain me sanity

because of the neutral collapse

of my body, the charged fire of my

immolation, the hatred

that I spew for the loved

ones of the world

who betrayed me, and who were never

human. (But they are.) No! What country made you? The same

as that of my pharmaceuticals? The same as that

of my imagined divinity, which knows no bounds

beyond the rabbit? And which knows no bounds

beyond the snake that keeps still

and quiet, beyond the Sun?

Silence Does Not Fear

I smile when I see these words.

Yet I am not Silent enough.

See the Silence
eclipse the Sun?

It must be as the heart does,
within the Ocean, of a Sea,
through sounds of *La Pintada*,

to make a whole meaning of it
which explodes on occasion

a self exploding vision

sticks and stones and leaves

this, I will be ready for. my body
opened with the books
of the worlds of the Silent

that I lick and read
with my tongue
of silence and sound

•

apart
and together

apart
and together

again

•

to dream myself
piercing
through hatred

into a snake again.

A red and black snake,
followed from the forms of light
that it breathes. The forms of light
in the eternal world of the blind,
that do not consider (and do not divide)
a link to be more
than flesh. Give up the view
that will not square the circle,

give it up
for the Quaternary
of every rain that harms you

I aim to be
a dissolving witness

a far away Wilderness
with a robust interface

made of light,
illusory, but made

to allow me to walk
in the world of roads

while in my heart
I have no roads
bewildered
in the midst of the planets
and their far away visits,
a self sustaining
Soul and Wilderness
One

with no time
and no Seeing

it breaks
into what seems to be

an absent world
without a world

except through the light

The Last Colors

snowed in
to the interior

mustard seed
grain of rice

formed
and unformed

radiations. A new
Sun

beyond the poles
makes a gift of itself

to the unconditioned

a gift
from no doctor.

It's always there
burning

through a song
of cognition. Planes

pass
on the content

of extermination.
The West

is ignorant
of the World.

But it believes
in its totem

despite the ground
that will never

be owned. I am not
from any direction

because I have folded in
on myself, to attract

wandering. There is no
wandering

profanity. There
I eclipse

my own visions
with the elderly

dreaming
on their own. At least

they dream. All planets
must know

that the Earth
now changes

toward what was promised
long ago

in not returning
to the absent

interior of life. Know
that our blood

makes a mark
on the world

to signify
a new mind

of the Moon.
To symbolize

through patterns
and affections, to

Save again
what the world was

Once

Mestizos de Avión

after Xul Solar

green after the show
tells me the impossible

grow for the fast clouds
as the border brings

your advantageous poverty
caused by you

let the exit word out, as each field
offers more to die with. go

and remember that violence
is a single shape in that cloud, go

with Western wandering
with the links toward each offering

to decide without answers
the conversation on the bus, the I.T.

suffrage and it's closed down
eyes, with no body — finishing

what you want me to love. but this
is not responsible for writing, or the cause

of a new metaphysics of the West —
Panamá. if you believe in the timeless,

the universal, the absolute zero of consciousness
veins through its cross there, delivers

what each form calls the fourth, the inside
job of dying for a bridge, to be a bridge

and Host what the highway, the jungle
remains to belong to your life. clear out

the vast exception, the transmission of a future
without secrets. you cannot avoid the offering scale

of integration, or one cannot be there
as the Sun was — waiting forever to be a Self

without ideas or feelings, with no body
but still human in some way, because the story leads there

to revolve around the promises and the bread
that each friend will erase you with, with the loss

of eating through balloons
and half remembered grains of sand, as they absolve

the Ocean and the Sea
and each hemisphere. Know that thinking

is not real with the advent of a lesser
kind of ground, and known with the other worlds

and other places revealed
to the tiniest minority

of Ocean life
and Sea life

and the poles. My head is given here
to belong not to a person, or to a voice,

or to a book, but the suffering
that is not cumulative   in a disease

of offering, in the redness of the kind of longing
that I plant into your chest, into your collapsed

lung, because your voice now
is not the color of the clouds

or of the sky, and it will not assume
that you know without the advent of armor

in these pictures, these religious worlds
off limits to me, as a Yogi of Panamá —

because of money, Rinpoche, because
of your ignorant purity

Mute and Sync

there are only reparations
to see there, only interfaces
made to endure the mob
in a plane that does not absorb
any light. remove the divine
from my false consciousness, remove it
so that I can be true. True in the sense
of the oceans, true in the sense
of my cruelty, which will never abandon you,
true in the sense of the attacks
that I witness at my own funeral, that they
will deliver the last blow, the parking lot
full of forgotten people, that they will see
that I am not standing, or laying down,
or even
in a shelter — the shelter now
that grows to devolve
into the stable
and ejected heart
of primordial death,
the death that equates cruelty
with the love of an animal. The aim
of this poem is to unwind
what you haven't seen
in you and me,
to turn inward and confront

the black sphere, that for so many
has caused fear and sorrow. I must be that,
that darkness, the hidden valley in the assault
of righteousness, the oppression that we feel
at the ends of severe
control and delivery, the ambush
under our bed
that says that you are not
to be trusted. That says that the game
is nocturnal and follows
the logic of the asteroids, as I write
with it, the mined iridium
from outer space
not to be confused
with another world
it is here. and it always will be. Stealth
beckons you, with the CIA
in your eternal
removal of historical page
swaps, the unknown
of where I become the shadow
to open the casket here again, and to slither
like worms and snakes
into the hiding place of darkness. What is it
about that darkness
that will not surrender
to your divine improvisations? Remove all entries
marked by kindness

and compassion in this book
and you will see what I am after. It is not
anger, it is not hatred, it is not lacking
in love, but it does remove the pretty bags
from your desperate shopping. It cannot be called
erasure, I am not fusing
the poles or trying to see
the goodness in you. I believe that we
have destroyed, over and over, and that there's
no room for us to talk
of love. Because it is
the most nontrivial thing
and because it must be stopped. Not the love
that you put a word for, but the eternal vagabond
of deception
that stratifies the looser ends
of our souls. Let me make this clear —
that I do not love as One. These insistences
will remain with the warmth and tenderness
that forms the ideal
and proceeds to murder
hundreds of thousands of people. I am that
darkness, so that we can better
remain alone, better execute in the light
what new world we are afraid of, what new
fundamentalism
here can show
to be flat, but dangerous. I am taking sides

in this war, as I pacify the machete
under my bed, a mark of my Latinidad
that holds you to the gruesome view
of death that many will return to, out of fascination
and not denial. We all die, and we all die again.
In this darkness, there is no place for the working
world,
there is no place for an engine
meant to cool off in a winter night. There is no
other side that you will aim for, as these
are not ideals. These are not the seeds
that will carry you further
through disaster,
but they are
the winds of these
that knock our shelters down and open
the real wound, the one we made ourselves,
the One
which is pure evil
in our hearts, to remember that it can be filled
by something
other than light. No saintly reader
can bring anything
to this poem. And no devil
will ever understand it.

Avian Moss

when everyone has gone home
I am home with her

fear the illusive
volcanic ash, that says

one more day
for the forgiven, as a shadow

net that holds us
from the cold, is attached

and forests
remind the electric sand

of the jobs that the wilderness
will offer, the climate

that I know, from the four eyes
of emptiness, and of the palms

remaining as she was
to see me — love is there, is here

and no fear can erase it
as a Sun is offered

for a blinding Word, a group
saddle that some live for

night and day
of owning nothing, night and day

for the time beyond
Of my life, that she

in her magical innocence
the city of her voice

and embrace, we knot ourselves
together   as we sleep, this heart

is given
always for her, always

for her cloudless rains
and weather, as the door

the door there
as we are, in the evolving climate

wherein   we knot ourselves
again   and remove

the fear, the fear of it
of losing

and of death. the fear of it
of losing

and of life. given to be
in the crossing   snow morning

for buses
we believe in, and sweat

Changing Deer

You gave me a name, and I move to you
to eclipse the sadness
of my temporary mind. Fear and anxiety
have proven false to me
as I insist on walking
through the darkness. No more
Quaternaries here, to mark the beginning
of wholeness
that I move through
the hurricanes that give us water.
The days are linked
to each wandering
forest, to beckon you
to live in our simple
and happy world
together, without number,
without anything
but the images of resurrection. These
images do not come from a book, they come
from the times you've proven to me
again and again, that there's love in the world
despite my certainty
that to love, I must be alone. "Gift"
isn't a big enough word
to describe what you've done
to my life,

it's a miracle
that I'm able to love at all, and through your
tenacity and faith
I know that now
and will always wear it
on every cell of my body
through each breath
I dissolve
to live
and love
with you

Noise of Eden

I remake the image
made of light

the thorns of synchronicity
wrapped in horses' hides

stretched across
the prairie fields,
of the restful ambulance

I tell a story
of the power of the bus
of Wilderness.

A siren

One

at the beginning
of the Salt.

Surrounded
by the redness
of the Sea.

the light of darkness, the light
of the invisible, through nomenclatures
of the harvesting bird
of the foams of contagion, of the excellent
distances which crowd us there
absorbing other levels
of the storms of the world, we form
the balls of infancy
and retrace our ancient
solitary travels
through the completed

Palms of prehistory.

we wander
the earth

as I now
wander

our plague
ridden Host.

I cross
a swinging bridge
which knows no water
except the sevens
that I count, here

and in the place I go to
which has no roads
and no mouth

a form is made by water
as the Ocean splits it

to bring the worlds together
of the light and of the clouds

the fusing tar on fire
of a unitive release

fumes for the soil
that breathes in

the occluded winds
of a morning's

indelible

electrified and silent
source of the field

Dangerous Cartoons

aggressions remain
televised, through the opposable

distances, and each of the eyes
neutral oceans and the natural

consequences, revolving
equations, tent songs as they

are finished and an approach
of limits and infinity, as seasons —

no tearful lines for the wilderness
and fits do not attune to it

as their ashes and removable
flights, a wrong arsenal

weakens you, does not shine
for the rain or One. let it

dissolve, as children, the seams
do not gather when winter

increases the evening lines, and the night
will remember as they remove

a Child. children here
sit the lesser and primordial

cranes, a time says, no longer
receives — as climate attachment

ends. Children, child — a storm
vanes and weather signs each light

ascent, what the flight will eat
nowhere for symbols, or a signal &

Symbol steams and an Ocean
divides. True, unity evades

bells and each one there is a horse
to reduce and resolve the stain

and witness, a crate of code
simulates and collapses — to a point

to Run through lightning
and segment each of the assassins

a spill of engagement
with trees, and with a seasonal case

of the torn, through its advantage as
a new night. shades of wire and a caress

in the alighted aisles
forward, through the tenses —

One does not aim
to be Two

Reason Is A Small White Cloud

I walk in the open
erasure of dreams,

shared

through the conflict
of an insect

pummeled

through the contradictions
of an endless alarm

tying the nodes
of entry

beside the impossible
beginning of light

within the unwelcome
proliferation of twins

of the invisible
network
of static attention

at the bottom
of the Sea. This error,

this single error

flows into an eclipse
of awakening, shaped

to find itself

tearing through shadows
that float us through

the morning of the moon's
communion
and congregation,

a union
of the unsung

and a collapse
of each word

ever released
onto the approximate

mapping
of the skies.

Scientific Break

my life is complete
like the moon

inside the earth. waking
through terror and holes

fade, forward on I see
and let go of cars

and swerve and lessen
through the snow, what do you look

that way, that offering, that silence.
what do you look when one says

light erases in the meadow
fish, and a butterfly

salt and the pier, the songs
still remove   the sky and earth

ejected within the force
of elevations, caves

as One burns   Not   the digitized
cost, a Host   sewn to it

as neutral and as a grown
circumference of roads

breathing in   the snow
in summer, Open as they

put the walking dust
and what happens when a call

is let loose. no talk
evokes what was, on the telephone

crate and cell, revolve and sell
to the upturned storms —

they don't know. they
hide shrunken entries

from the tops of a network
and seal, and realize the resizable

to remain as other doors
delimit and seize

the bottom. rain when it is   the rain
servile surveillance   and categorical lines

fuse what the station
in its recovery, and destruction

floods   one at a time
the real action of silence

and wet trees, and the sunrise
of being captured

for nothing. a dog
rips   through its casket

VM

stay to the air, the removable
eclipse of your Sun. one way
to integrate the lost message, the box
of targets that will serve to reveal
each market value of the feeling, the round
magnet sending the moon toward you
in the event of a single night, the one with the ears
of the proposition, the Sun wall and the enormous
guillotine, the increasing dust of the wandering
cow, through town, through the insert
that the fine tuning of your water gourd, your
many headed lines that solve the earth and move
the hands off their hidden places, that puts blood
on the removable exception, as there is one
to the winter that stalks and which is the night,
folding and climbing the state of internal
Wilderness, it is there, the interface of light,
the road-less place that makes me walk
toward the roads, and then one has to speak
and there was a horse, and more, many of them,
so long ago, as I learned to breathe
not knowing that I would find it there again,
in black, not knowing that the horse would arrive
to segment and negotiation
of the channels of the night

and to replace it's One distance and the arrival
here and now, the arrival that says her wind
is the nocturnal, the riot facing the calmness
and suicide of the finished, the engine will not
start, and there is the horse again, and then
the breathing that I've tried. So I am still a victim
of the shallow breath. I did not learn my lessons
well, but I am alive. And the obstacles have replaced
their messages with the long barefoot walk again,
that they see there what news will travel to its sound
and to reveal it and receive it, and to ride to the One
Canal as they are, to it there, and they are to it, in
the abundant greenery, I travel to… to be home,
to sleep and to undo the wire from her sign. And there is
a kind solvent, each one a remembering place, as they tunnel
to the four corners and the four forces of the planet
to make One. And one has seen that there is no real
engine to it, one to eliminate
the fascination of her religion,
as I am not. To see there once with it in the time of her
walking. There is a secret darkness there, the arrival of it
makes all the world a fearful place, without the talking
and one is seeing through that, and one is Silent
in the corporate Totalitarian state, which I defeated
in Silence. The poems from that time are underground,
and there is the real sense of it, to empty the garden
and speak to their One action committee, and the seen
is broken to remake One to the air as there is their count

in the finished appraisal that has
the undone there

in the segmented place and the long light of their walk
and then there is the Seen, the Seen as there is one to speak
and the tongue there is remembered for its fallow
rain river and the more that one has it to arrive in the soon
to be remaining in the patch of its puppet. Then one
describes what her tonic and the cold material of the glass
and the weather to know it in these combinations
of its allowable tender and one to the night. And then
there is one to the air that one has in their time of it, in this
and the segment has remade itself, and it might sleep in the
winter air, and the air of it is solid to be behind the past
and one time to their only saying it as NINE
and as the collapsing foot and trail of it to the warm
and the opposable regard and the time of its silence and they
decided to be there, It is one there in the light of its numerical
science

and then they see there that one has the mark of the field
to remain. One has to carve it to see it. And one has the less
engineer and the less architect and the less round type for her
exceptional rain, and the science to replace the motor in its
domain, and the arrival there of one segment of the lock,
and the time for her serious one to be and then to be and then to see
and to arrive to its place to make one on the ground and become
the One thing as it is to remember and relate her sound in the forest

and then one has there to be it
in the magnetic time and the Seeing
as the forest is there to see and to bring the light to undo
in the opposite place

Cyberecology & the World

light and water make life. things will change with the birth of the hydrocephalic computer.

Searching for Satellites

the news
is released

for the secret
of worlds, I reach

the end
of my laughter

and breathe
to the night sky

a periodically
interrupted song

to reach the forest
of my refuge, here

where the lights are
where one dissolves

and appears. to see the hidden
files of your mind

and listen

listen

as I cross the road
to find the fox

of the funeral home's
bewildering delight

where there is laughter
marked by a mysterious

blinking light

that the occluded
erase the sun with, and I've lost

my heart
for the present moment, as I fear

it is one more day
to see others walk

in the dark morning
of imposters

and timeless life. I say
farewell to you, my love

as I enter the darkness
to be with you

in our morning kisses, and see
that we shall never part

your heart

as the Sea was parted
as the world collapses

and we say 'yes'
to the fearsome light

Song Wish

we both say it
through the undivided

moon

more volcanoes
will respond to the light

who reads
but the disappeared?

who understands
but the people of light? who

will reach the Sea
and cross   to the Ocean?

who knows
what the morning   will deliver

before night? before
the eclipse   of cameras, before

the impossible   quaternary
which allows me to breathe

through you. friends, there is
no train, here, to deliver us

taintless water
to drink. only the guard

will see it. but we shall never
be apart, I see it now. nothing

can divide love
and nothing

can truly live
without it

●

see what the winds
will see

here
see it here

A Shelter of the Sun

there is no dream world
that will dissolve
for less than the future. I cannot fly. And once,
there were animals,

and plants thriving from her touches
and the love of her broadening song. They
have captured the elephant,
which feels remorse at separation
the one remaining
as it is small and without a neutral
casing of the shop. No more returns,
as these will not provide a page
to see with. No intrusion, here, no hand,
no season, no tunnel

folding in on itself

that the formless find with its song. The song
hustles what the night offers, it cakes
our obscene answers, the erased time of it
to reveal and multiply with the sounds
of a zeroing
attachment, the road
where each symbol
of the primordial seems

to not receive, will not bound the world
with a wire. Given that magic, that the turn
found inside the miles away

the houses away
the ferns away

the cities away
the stars away

the fields and fields away

Give me hope, the arrival of their standing
I groveled — zero sum for the entire
radio memorization. Give me hope then, that the eye
will not follow, that the saddle will elevate
a door, a field, one of the deer
to their features of light. Give me standing
that dreams will not be misused, that the iron
of the poles
and each of the replies, each of the threads
will exit, They will endure
through the aftermath of one of the points
of the human that I cannot touch. Give
me the reason
for forgetting
each of the exceptional nights

and he dreams
and he dreams terrifying dreams
and their fire will extinguish as these borders, these flowers
will bring the onslaught of signs. There is no real exception
as they love, as they reclaim their homes
and the sky is trembling, to it, to the dream
to escape and sleep. And there is one humanity
one in the skies finished with a revolving
migration, as it is not effective to be practical there
purely so

I drink from the well
of light, from the exceptional star
and I sit and I sleep
to remain one with the earth, as my silence
will equip you
to turn after the constellation
it sees. There is no more to reveal
in our encapsulating shell
to the end of nightmares
the end of its song, the buried intersection
as they are one, as us. Do not make it right, for silence
is silence   it is not and it is
it is silence, give it silence to amount to
an Open heart. Give it silence there to wrestle
with 12 dreams. The 12 dreams of the event
and singing
and their singing is not filled
with the earth, but it is. It is filled with the earth.

I give you silence
like the palms

of my seven years
of completion.

I give you the hope
of a starless sky,

the blackened pines
that will shelter us.

I give you the love of remission,
of the coma

which settles the futile
conversation.

I give it all to you as light, here, in the eclipse
of my shadow. I've entered the dark to illuminate
and it is long before me. Long before numbers.
Long before a silent cave, as it settles to agree
and One is not the open field

it is there
it is there as love

the field is there as love

a source of it

Christ of Jaén

after Borges

I am not here

as a man
as a tree
or as a rabbit

Terror does not comfort me
and I avoid
the dreams of the world

for that, I am sorry.

Not because of the vitriol
of comfort, but to see
that the Oceans believe
in my mind, but I
do not. And not because
of the feelings of the wandering
flag, you so declared, you
on the bricks
in offering. I ask

that no one sleep tonight
so that we can see together
what the real dream is

that there is no easy way
to become like the light
to become the divine
which has forgotten us. there is no
plan for the efforts of the music

that destroys the fevers
of cartoons. And I seek,
here, here with the thorny rose
of darkness, as I walk
to release the clouds
and allow the water
to find me, in forgiveness
and in clarity. Please remember

that the television
is not real

that computers
are ritual
and magic objects
meant for the light
of the heart, and
that they will disappear

like the I Ching

and that our comforts
destroy our dreams

with an exit
from all

the forms of love

SNAKE VISION: A POETICS

The following poetics statement partly grounds itself in a discussion of how I've made meaning of my life given that I am severely bipolar, having been diagnosed as such since my early twenties. However, much more motivates me to write, draw, and paint than questionable psychology. I do not intend to romanticize mental illness, but aim to move toward integration. As Jackson Mac Low points out, we are not always integrated — it is an ideal and a limit to move toward as we remain human. Some of the experiences discussed are easily life threatening, so I don't aim to treat them lightly, but instead of always pathologizing, my intention is to move toward being grounded and whole without that warning and limiting gesture always being around the corner. And, I was interested in art before these events and know that these experiences do not make me an interesting poet or anything other than someone aiming to live fully.

Snake as poetic form — (somewhat in recent work): start with the head — spiritual knots to be unraveled in the body/spirit of the poem. Sometimes near repetition as scales repeat. Unraveling, loosening, opening… tie a snake in a knot and it will unravel itself and glide away smoothly… psychic/spiritual knots dissolving.

Panamá — geographically shaped like a snake — the present moment (bridge between the past and the future) — place of many fishes — the bridge of the world, the crack of the egg of the world — always in between

Acausality — It all happens at once. I saw that this was true in my first manic (psychotic) phase. 20 years later I saw this confirmed in Dzogchen. Later, I found it discussed by Jung and other writers. Only the mind needs time? Writing is an effort to get to this state.

numbers especially meaningful to my poetics — 1, 2, 3, 4, 5, 7

1 — higher unity
2 — twin (*el huerco* — our twin appearing as we prepare for death — helping us with the affairs of the world) — stereophonic, duality
3 — third way, beyond duality, an alternative kind of thinking, trinity, past binary, isthmus, integration
4 — 4th dimension — beauty, time, intuition — the four parts of an intersection or cross — I was a 4D programmer

5 — age of psychological completeness, I was in Panamá, psycho-logically completely Panamanian (though culturally Panamanian-American)

7 — the seven directions (north, south, east, west, up, down, center -0). I arrived to this country at the age of seven (though I was born in Oregon to Panamanian parents while my father was going to college at Oregon State, we returned to Panamá by the time I was six months old. Spanish was my first language and I did not begin learning English until I arrived to Delaware at age 7). Milarepa says that "mind has no east or west."

First manic phase: after traveling for a year on $2K (reading Henry Miller, Kerouac,...) — (rode the trace of a lemniscate with center at Bloomington, IN throughout United States, Mexico, and Canada — 15K miles in 6 months in a '72 Plymouth Duster I bought for $500), then on to Europe and Morocco, mostly hitchhiking and living in my tent (especially meaningful was my visit to the Atlas Mountains in Morocco — Tleta Ketama, hundreds of miles of marijuana fields! The people throughout Morocco were by far the most indigent I'd ever encountered, as well as, by far, the most generous. Being there was like having walked into someplace biblically radiant. I also hitchhiked the entire coast of Spain and some of its interior — and other places.) — then returned to graduate school in Mathematics, first case of verifiable tilt — to the Math Class I was teaching, "read 4.1" (walked in, wrote on board, and left), next day, "read and understand 4.1" (walked in, wrote on board, and left) — I felt I needed to return from traveling to learn to write and to give graduate study in Math another chance. But it became impossible to translate my storm of traveling onto graduate studies and my first attempts at writing. I felt too much energy to concentrate on such a small, focused place.

Manic phases are by a million miles and lifetimes the most beautiful experiences of my life as well as the most terrifying. Apocalyptic/revelatory — much of their meaning remains secret, permeated in my body and soul, only to arise in small pieces in my poems, saturated into the form, hence no longer causing imbalance in a world of time, now becoming more and more a part of the everyday world. Building a world of vision, firmly planted in the ground. Everything has been revealed to me. I know nothing. We shrink to be ourselves, only because we live in time (or I do). The problem with revelation is to see it as a self/i. What is being revealed, or at least in my case, what was revealed was too big for me to comprehend given my life at that point. This is probably still the case. Not to make an argument for knowing something over someone else, necessarily, as a result of these experiences, though I do think, ultimately, that they give me the advantage of seeing the illusory nature of certain things that most people cling to (eg. being "smart" — especially in IT; this is not to make an argument against the value of intelligence, just that what most people see as being intelligent is just fast eye blinking and fast talk). What does one really gain by seeing something that belongs to everyone and everything and all — and nothing/no one?

Bridging dichotomies — coming to terms with the visionary/spiritual qualities of my natural state of hallucination — 0/1, true/false, rational/irrational, the hemispheres, sun/moon, the stereophonic, real/virtual, random/purposeful, private/public, earth/sky, mind/body — "all problems of life are problems of harmony" — Sri Aurobindo — how does an effort toward harmony come to terms with amazing dissonant music such as Merzbow, etc? Dissonance seems vital too. My writing has become a kind of Yoga, a putting together. The snake (*culebra*) is a yogic animal; the bicycle is a yogic machine.

Hole in time — eternity— inhabiting the plane of body language and ignoring/bypassing information control — aiming to walk through to freedom in all possible contexts — not always there, but have been, especially during manic phases, in a heightened sense

I am the snake — initial vision of transformation in the mirror (25 years ago — one of my first manic visions — I viewed in horror as I saw myself turn into a snake — only now am I able to make meaning of this) — mirror shattered as I pounded both sides of it — small star trek insignia scar in the middle of my chest (from a shard of the mirror)

1st manic blowout (22 years old) — took things that were symbolic of my life — my dad's coat (his violence), my 3 piece suit (my unwanted and forced aim for the working world), my Math books (my failed attempt at "reason"), my refrigerator (my fear) — put them all in a dumpster near my trailer and set it on fire. I hallucinated and barely slept for a month. I walked twelve miles barefoot and found horses to learn to breathe from, desperately trying to figure out a way to remain on earth. Birds flew at synchronous times.

EVERYTHING was hyper-meaningful: A Goth friend's bat earring signifying that she and I were to fly through some mysterious night, the way the garbage cans were lined up on the side of the road signified that the entire town was ready — the following morning — to join me in my/our vision, gestures indicated the secret life of the spirit in the everyday, cracks in the sidewalk accurately and perplexingly signified something to be solved at another time, paper flying by was purposeful and random — even that signified some kind of musical accompaniment to my realizations, the wind moved in such a way as to be understood by me in my new mind — that the magic of the old world was returning. I felt I was being somehow called to save, as a sort of messiah, and that we were all needing to take on this kind of role…I was not the only one…that I'd arrived at a final transformation, that absolutely everything had become symbolic and hyper-meaningful (in many, many layers), that we were entering a new world. Partly my writing is a way to pace the surfacing of the meanings (infinite) of these experiences.

I was locked up in a jail cell in Bloomington, IN, for a few days. I struggled to get free and so the guards tore my clothes to shreds. They gave me an orange jumpsuit to wear. They put me in a small room watched by video camera. I had just returned from traveling for a year, the freest time of my life, only to find myself there. I paced myself by making miniscule steps across the cell — MINISCULE — so that it took me hours to walk from one side of the cell to the other. All the while my head was spinning out of control. I saw some horrible things. My life became redefined, as if I was being taught an important lesson by a gentle but also ruthless force → I had been a science experiment — someone put together by science sent out as an experiment to live what was meant to be a normal childhood, normal by standards of superhuman tribulation. The important thing was that I was to learn to believe that I was a part of humanity, though the secret was that ultimately, in some mysterious way, I was not. I had grown up son of a prostitute and a pimp. Abuse was rampant in my parents, and, ultimately, I saw them die in the corner of my jail cell. These were not the stories I "grew up" with, completely. (In what I accept as my 'real' life, my mother was not a prostitute, and my father was not a pimp. But their difficulties made for mine.)

It became clear to me that there were several threads of narratives to explain my life and that I could not resolve them. I aimed to focus on the truth, in all of its multivalence and movement. I'm not sure what level of detail is useful here. Suffice it to say, for now, that they transferred me to the mental hospital, where they locked me up in a white room. I banged loud on the door, as a heart in an egg. 9 of them came to tie me down on the bed. I struggled and it was a while before they could get me down. Once they overcame me, I shit in my pants in revenge. "Eat shit," I thought. They tranquilized me as I was strapped down on all fours, and then they left the room. I was able to free myself of one leg and one arm. When I awoke, I found myself, terrified but strong, in the shape of a swastika. Not being in any way a Nazi, I took this to mean that the line between an ancient benevolent symbol and a symbol of horror is thin. It is only recently that I have taken the meaning of this symbolic event in my life to be in harmony with the Kuna swastika, which represents the Octopus that created the world. On entry into the dazed life of psychotropic meds and the beginnings of therapy, I was initially diagnosed as schizophrenic, but responded to drugs that indicated that I was bipolar. The line has been thin. In San Francisco, CA, years later, it was pointed out to me that I have enlarged brain ventricles, a sign of schizophrenia, so this remained unclear to me for a long time. Though recently I've learned that schizophrenia is much more degenerative than bipolar disorder, so it seems the current diagnoses is accurate. I am currently on a moderate dose of a single medication (after many years of up to 6 meds at a time), Zyprexa, which is used for both bipolars and schizophrenics.

I have not had recourse to family support throughout these experiences, which have lasted on and off for 25 years. At one point I was on Social Security Disability for 3 years. My true family lives in the present eternal moment. It is only through them that I love.

How to integrate these experiences that for life's sake were pathologized and which at the same time, often have strong spiritual/poetic resonances? How to make meaning of my life instead of devaluing, instead of having vast parts of it remain outside of the life of the world? Part of the answer is to let things flow through and not to hold on to anything. This is why Buddhism has become so important to me (though I am not exclusively Buddhist) — remaining on the ground, balanced, aiming to breathe calmly. Useful here is a line from Joron's *The Sound Mirror*: "Silence, like poetry, is neither true nor false." → Mania, like poetry, is neither true nor false.

(I am not addressing the depressive side of bipolar disorder in these notes)

Of my books so far, tentatively and not exclusively:

Os — my first balance of energy in poem form — by definition: a bone and/or a mouth — shaky tension of poles. I died in this book and made my first steps in my new life.

Counter Daemons — way of seeing. Much of the imagery from my manic phases is here, as plain as possible.

bicycle — way of being. I rode every day except 3 or 4 days a year for 4 years (not on Fridays) 20 miles a day/night. I rode through all kinds of weather. I communed with the landscape, the weather, the pier, the lake, the sun, the moon, the ground... the bicycle may serve as a metaphor for bridging all duals — North America/South America, with Panamá as the isthmus... (two distinct wholes brought together to make a greater whole, moving toward the number 3), ...

culebra — (current project — in two sections, 0 and 1) — way of knowing. all tercets (tercets, in my view, among other things, imply circles, loops, or circuits — as in the appearance, abiding, and return of thoughts and of sparks of the soul). Uroboros — Neumann's *The Origins and History of Consciousness* — my fight with the dragon

Aurélia was my dear grandmother's name. I named her "Malela" when I was an infant — always naming. Nerval's *Aurélia* is also the story that most closely relates to some of this ("Dream is second life."), though what is described in *Aurelia* I went through in a single day, and that story was a minimal representation of what I've experienced overall.

Artaud does not speak to me of my experiences, though I am interested in his writing. It's difficult for me to believe that he was ever crazy. He seems more like a mystic and philosopher. He escaped psychology — "an athlete of the heart."

I've had 12 major psychotic phases. As I call them, my 12 apostles of nothing (to borrow from Badiou, of whom I know nothing): What to do with a messianic impulse that aims to be common, saturating form so as to keep it on the ground. Each phase lasts at least a month, and once, up to a year (in San Francisco, CA) — a total of about 3 years in mental hospitals/half way houses, 2-3 years of hallucination, much much stronger than any drug

I saw the recreation of the universe in a final phase, of 3 elements — black, white, and clear — carbon, sand, and water? Jackson Mac Low was one of the main spirits of the final recreation.

Psychic communication — vulnerability/vibration — the hole of the heart that aims to be full — stopping missiles with my mind. We can read minds, but how does one understand what one reads? I walked into a KFC in Chicago with a key gently twisting in the air; the clerk threw bills of money in the air; chicken nuggets outside in the parking lot were representative of a cyberspace knot, of a nuclear standoff. I helped to redistribute state secrets and to find a balance of power. With cyberspace as a new psychic realm, will it be psychic before we're all ready? (Parallel universes are close by, only need a small shift to get there, and there are correspondences, ties, links between, ways to move things in another world from here and vice versa). What protects us from this volatility?

Psychic knots tie us all together. We're tied in knots in groups of threes and fours. The secret is how to help the energy move through these knots. These social knots are different than psychic/spiritual knots. Psychic/spiritual knots are meant to be untied and released. Social/psychic knots are useful and meant to be traveled.

Listening to and understanding the birds

Learning to breathe from the horses (after walking twelve miles barefoot)

Learning from the weather

To learn from Saint Francis of Assisi as Hardt/Negri discuss him, the new revolutionary, and to come to terms with their "multitude" … the basics of knowing animals and how that might have political/spiritual implications — not overtly political, from this angle? Sometimes, but from the other side — the many animals of my life (220 rabbits… snakes…7 lovebirds… many others) — animals need us to speak softly to them — snakes make circles, rabbits make cylindrical tunnels

Talking from the other side of the word

Cyborg — we are all already there. If, as Christian Bök notes, poets should aim to be understood by computers — I disagree, partly, nonconceptual more relevant than ever — what is the nonconceptual? Always beyond — time bound as we aim to conceptualize everything? But, form is emptiness, AND emptiness is form. The cyborg has been an ongoing theme of my manic phases, the thin line between real life and virtual life (this before I'd ever heard of cyborg theory, and even now I do not understand Donna Haraway and rarely read science fiction). I expect that cyberspace will be like a telescope/microscope and that using it we will find new worlds. I have already led a squadron of cyberspace flyers through the initial minefields years ago, when I was asked to teach a class on electronic bulletin boards, so some of us are prepared…to feel the horror of not being able to determine whether a being is flesh or machine, and to move past that horror. (I was a Peoplesoft programmer — technology as poetry, code within poems — to rehumanize and at the same time acknowledge a new cyber/? way of being)

Countering dehumanization — internal AND external — at the same time coming to terms with possible cyborg future — pathology as both dehumanization and lifesaver? (only truth value makes it either one?)

A new kind of Yoga is needed to allow the advanced cyborg to succeed in being human.

The cockroach has an evenly distributed nervous system. One can crush its head and it will walk away, decentralized nervous system → decentralized poetics — no need for centers of power? no reason for centralized understanding of a given poem? web — noosphere — supermind?

Seeing all the ancient animals returning

People take on a multitude of faces — many are ancient Indian heros/heroines returning in the final days (for a moment).

If, as Pound says, all times are contemporaneous, I conclude that all worlds are coexistent here as well

I found a children's playground in San Francisco, CA, and buried a deck of tarot cards there in the sand. The gesture was meant to have children recreate my life.

When I wander in my manic phases (before reaching the half way house or hospital), I wander long. For the last fifteen years, when I've wandered in these states, I've anchored myself by sticking a knife in the floor of my apartment — a special knife. It was my father's. The knife of the devil, as I grew up knowing him, and though the devil has his horrifying aspects, with which I am very familiar, as I am his son, he also has his playful & loving aspects: demon/devil as figure of carnavál — a lighter, more playful, less polarized interpretation in Panamá than here... the devil as Indigenous/African interpretation?

Carnavál — Diablito Dulce

Silence, learning from silence — the ringing in our ears that is the decentralized nervous system, the inner sound in all of us, as Cage heard in the silence chamber. That high pitched sound is loud everywhere now — it is the link between us and the seasonal metallic sound of the cicada, which brings on the cyborg

MOLA — fabric art done by the Kuna Indians of Panamá, usually made in pairs as the Kuna believe everything arrives in the world in pairs — I am unknown to the Kuna but aim to help them, as I was raised with many of their Molas on the walls of our home — cloud systems transporting the souls from below the line to here — making signs for them (and all, from all of Latin America) to arrive. They will arrive who are not us. — signs are everywhere — Burroughs — "READ THE SIGNS." a hyper overflowing of meaning — learning to swim through that — MOLAS becoming to me what the Chinese ideogram was to Pound (vibration — to lead back to Sri Aurobindo, red and black sound and vulnerability — to lead back to Lorca's black sound,… animals, duality, MOLAS always there)

I've heard of a National Geographic article which discusses a strong sense of ESP among the Kuna

"Truth is the death of intention" (Walter Benjamin) — exploring what that might mean. — intention in regard to meaning. I may intend to write a poem but not totally intend its meaning. — is this oracular? if so, so what? ORACLE PROGRAMMING (I was an Oracle programmer) — I'm not entirely there — intention implies time and causality — synchronicity and acausality agree with Walter Benjamin, also with José Lezama Lima. How does this line affect truth value of manic phases? Part of the problem (huge) is gauging the intention of others → paranoid etc . → ego must be strong and healthy before aiming to grow spiritually — intention must be strong and healthy before aiming for truth as Benjamin describes it?

Hallucination, as I've experienced it, is without intention

The walls of the basement of the house I grew up in are covered with many layers of graffiti, in English and in Spanish, accumulated over the years while my sisters and I and my cousins lived there, made by us and friends of ours. I remember once seeing a note written on one of the walls, a few years after it was written, and realizing that the person who wrote it had died shortly after graduating from high school, shortly after having written the graffiti. Gradually, this became true of more and more of the graffiti, more and more of its writers/creators passing away. The walls are rich and they remain, raw and powerful as my first and continuing experience with what writing/drawing can do.

I have been deeply influenced by Language Writing, though feel the need to reframe what I'm doing without it.

Lezama Lima's image — cosmic writer of place — symbolizing grammatically — baroquely — unify — *mestizaje* — "The knowing that is not ours and the not knowing that is ours form for me true knowledge." — "The penetration of the image into nature engenders supernature." — "Liberation from time is the most unrelenting constant of supernature." — "I attain the tetractis, the number four, God." — "The image is the reality of the invisible world." — "Poetry… is the image attained by the man of resurrection." — "I try in my system to destroy Aristotelian causality by seeking a poetic state of unconditionality" — "… the poetry of a return to magic spells, to rituals, to the living ceremony of primitive man."

Vallejo and his indianness and solitude — again, *mestizaje* — silence — numbers — compassion — emotion — "the whole song/squared by three silences" — "And don't strike 0, which will be so still/until it wakes the 1 and makes it stand" — "a trine between the two" — "Armor-plate this equator, Moon." — "it ends up being all numbers,/ the whole of life" — "in the insane search/for the known one" — "Make way for the new odd number/pregnant with orphanhood!" — "doubt your excrement a few seconds" — "There is a place that I myself know/in this world, no less,/we will never reach" — "But the place that I myself know,/in this world, no less,/sought pace with its opposites." — "My eternity has died and I am waking it."

Often I find that I am settled with a poem when, while reading it aloud, I feel that I air out a profound wound, located throughout my body, but especially in the area around my heart and my throat. This is a very raw and visceral experience which defies easy explanation. In this sense, vulnerability is nonconceptual, and I aim at a cosmic vulnerability. It's as if I need to go beyond any capacity I have to conceptualize in order to get to any truly healing energy in my work. I cannot heal myself without going beyond myself, and from there, allowing myself to be rearranged from what I am at the present moment, letting the light in which is also beyond me. I need to continually find new ways of airing the wound because my windows to it always close in time. And so I do not believe in stylizing (conceptualizing) uncertainty. This fact has no clear implication as to the needed form of a given poem. And poems sometimes take on this quality for me after some time, or the quality can be otherwise time dependent. A nearly impossible aim is to get past this time dependency.

Laura Riding's truth (both near and far)

Pathology, within this context, permeates thoroughly through the imagination, thinking and feeling. An enormous amount of effort is required to let these areas grow and live freely while being treated for bipolar disorder. This is the case even with the best doctors I've encountered. Once, I was kept in the hospital for an extra week directly as a result of showing one of my doctors a poem I wrote that was slightly disjunctive. More recently I showed my doctors an early version of these *Snake Vision* notes, to which they responded with alarm and suggesting extra sessions (I calmed them down). My impulse is often to share my work, if I feel a bridge with the person, no matter who it is. I continue to learn to move in small steps. My largest leaps are yet to come as a result. Even within these constraints, I have managed, ultimately, not to compromise my aesthetic. Most doctors are not interested in art or spirituality, a serious limitation on their part. Similarly, most Buddhists I've encountered are not interested in art or in other spiritual paths. Only the imagination is real? Buddhism has no real answer for that. And neither does psychotherapy.

Lorca's duende? vulnerability, transrational imagery, earthiness, confronting death, demonic energy to struggle against (as he called it — the 'black sound')— Panamanian Folk music → Agustín Rodriguez, Fito Espino, Yin Carrizo, Décimas, *pindín…* these are to me what Cante Jondo was to Lorca + the true Cante Jondo is powerful to me as well → iPod (shuffle mode) = collage consciousness

Henry Flynt — using folk rhythms to make mantic drones

Agustín Rodriguez (from Panamá) — YO SOY TODO LO QUE AMO (I am everything that I love) / "Amanecer Campesino" — to wake up as a campesino, amazing album

I arrived at prehistory and relived some moments within those worlds. I could see the mechanism that made all times exist together. Speaking to one person, I spoke to many others. Finitude was left behind. Voices carried in a timeless echo. This moving through of energy helps in not being saddled, and paralyzed, by any fixed truth value? … How to find truth in motion (and stillness).

To find one's first place of dying, to stand there, and to guide for others on their way from there (language) — is language the first place of dying? Is it the imagination? Is it freedom? (I was taken to jail briefly for directing traffic on a busy highway in San Francisco, CA — where I saw that I was carrying this out in the final moments of the world).

All the while knowing the absolute evil one is capable of — beauty/terror

Forgiveness and what that does for freedom

I am the snake
I wander
through the corn fields
of your mind

Circles tattooed on my palms are anti-stigmata, and the wholeness of my life, its revolving. When my palms come together, everything stops

Hannah Weiner's jaguar from *The Fast* tattooed on my right arm

I confronted an army of therapists and won. They helped me in my fallen state. I won in terms of living in a multitude of worlds.

Making the smallest steps, infinitely traveling toward a broadly inclusive spirituality, outside the cell — learning from the syncreticism and errors of Christianity in Latin America — also knowing that in some ways our time is limited, and we are limited (? — not if in touch with the mind, with eternity?) and so what does that mean in terms of a single approach? — how can writing/art be a spiritual practice? Should it be? How can it not be? How to gain the infinite and remain on the ground? That's where the largest part of my learning of the spiritual is, to remain grounded.

I was raised by an Indian woman — Julia Chacón.

I was born with very large black and red moles covering my body (my mother says they were the size of strawberries and that she and my father were horrified to see them). They were removed soon after birth. Another complication of my birth was a double hernia — troubled by the dual from the start. MOLAS are mostly black and red and are usually made in pairs. Strawberry/Blackberry fields forever? — What to do with these kinds of strange truths and parallels? Not everything strange is a manifestation of psychosis. Where's the line? (There is no line).

I am not like you/I am like you.
I see/I am seen.
I arrive/You arrive.

red & black → on & off — & flesh (the third)

light is the line, dark is the breath.
red is the line, black is the breath,
marks on the flesh of the isthmus.

how does it all suddenly make perfect sense? <u>everything</u>

"Dance, you monster, to my soft song." — Klee

Mind imagines reason. QED

What imagines the eternal?

A way of poetry to make sense of life.

To commune. To move. To be still.

Horses of Insight

for Peter O'Leary

I walked the woods
after breathing quietly
and seeing everything
dissolve…

Four times I saw the horses:

one black stallion,
with a lightning bolt
of white
streaking down its forehead,
and two brown mares.

Each day I sang to them
and showed them each
of my hands.

The first day all of them
came to the fence
to share with me their origins.

The second day
they were already at the fence
when I arrived, to fill
the balls of light inside.

The third day
a black cat
with a lightning bolt
of white
on its chest, came and played
with me as the horses
breathed quietly
at a distance
far away, but also
on the inside
of my heart. They were

at the dividing line
between each breath
and carried my light
from one breath

to the next. The cat
was happy
as it was the night
where morning
must be born. The last day

the two mares waited
apprehensively for me
as the black stallion breathed
upon the fence

all things
must cross,
and which divides
him
from the mares.

I sang to them each
day, and each day
showed them each
of my hands. And on the last

day, I fulfilled my promise to them
that they would be
the horses of my dream, that I would
ride with them through all the lands
that now arrive
inside the breath. And as I said goodbye

and left, I walked away
and further on
I heard the hoof steps in the trees
I thought were deer
but it was them.

The horses
as they see me now
revealed
to be with them

Bridge of the World

this morning I went to the doctor
and talked to him about this move

on New Year's Eve I had trouble connecting
my thoughts on Sade and reason

we rang in the New Year
with Miriam Makeba's *Africa*

I'd noticed that my inner life
had expanded, and that I was having trouble

thinking through it. The doctor said that Geodon
would loosen my thinking — I noticed

that I'd been moving through life for 10 years
in a Zyprexa mold. thought control, at its best,

like a sonnet. I do not feel invaded
by the television that I never see. Brenda made me

feel more loved than ever this morning, as my thoughts
expanded. Last night, in the slow cooker, I made

Lamb and Goat curry — amazingly good. I'd thought
to send Joel, and Peter, and Michael an email

letting them know of my transition, but did not. The consequences
of this transition could be catastrophic. I feel more loving toward Brenda

than ever. I could die, or worse. As I meditated today
my books to the left of me seemed packed and dense

against the wall. Soon, Chuck will be here
to play chess upstairs. I told the doctor this morning

that the philosophy and religion of the cyborg
have not yet been written. My

poetry
has just begun. I am

a Fourth Form,
though not as Dodie saw it. Together,

we can belong in this world. Artaud
arrived at the double

as I have. We share more in common
than I'd known before last night. I need less sleep

than before, and I sleep better
and am more rested. I feel sad and cheated

that I need to rely on drugs
so completely. I wonder about Paul Bowles' stories.

I need to reach out
to others

through this. The doctor, this morning, said
that I was enlightened, but not

quite there — somehow — I can't remember
how. I doubt he knows

what he means by "enlightenment." I felt far away
from my sister yesterday, when she called. Michael

talked to me of Christ's
tenderness. I feel tender in this moment. Over

and over I feel that words
do not represent me. I am not

sure what that implies of my intentions
in using them. Yesterday, Brenda and I saw

the Warhol show of the last ten years
of his life. There seemed to have been hope

to live meaningfully in capitalism then. ~~~~~~~ The waves
of this beginning, the new life of my mind

is settling. It's been a while since I've written. I've decided
to mark my continuing with the seven tildes above. And I added

a title tonight, *Muerto Vecino*, after Zizek's dubious interpretation
of Kierkegaard's neighbor, and because of the funeral home

across the street. My thinking has changed, my being has changed,
I am more alert and more engaged in thinking through the world.

And I am able to speak better. I don't know what this means
about who I am. I try not to feel let down that for so much of my life

I've been restrained by psychotropic drugs. Before Zyprexa it was even
worse, with up to 6 meds, as I've said over and over to friends. I feel

the need to make clear what my obstacles have been. Not for pity,
a little for pride, but also for hope. If I can do that, then maybe I can help

someone not suffer so much, like Brenda. I replaced the kitchen faucet
this past weekend. It makes me very happy that I was able to do it

successfully, without ever having been handy before in my life, and after
spending most of my life disdainful of being practical in that way. What a joy

to make Brenda so happy. I don't know how much longer I will live,
and have often thought, recently, that it would be tragic if I died anytime

soon, but that it's imperative that I accept death when it arrives, after
affirming life as fully as I can. It's too easy, and stupid, to be simplistically

oppositional. And to not know that people can ruin anything, but
that the substantial things have value of themselves, is foolish. I don't want to stop

at my own ignorance and lack of forbearance. I don't believe in the West
on its own. As Michael says, the only thing that makes sense here

is love. I have everything I could possibly ever want or need for now. More books
will come, more music too. And love is immeasurable

when it's real. I am so grateful to have more waking time
on the weekends. I plan on making breakfast for Brenda

every Saturday and Sunday that I can
from now on. Early. I see gardens in the future of our household.

And I wonder about a Great Spirit. What does the name matter? I see the stones that live
without water. I see the smoke that cleanses my vision, and a network of consciousness,

with each node another, on and on that way to the depths. My thinking will never
grasp it all

because of that recursively created network of interior life. My thinking stops
then, barely able to contain the spherical and vast darkness

from which all light arises. That's why what I see is dark. It is brilliant
in its darkness. Like onyx and flint. I can only talk around what I've seen

the past couple of weeks. It reframes, completely, the rest of my creative
life and the rest of my days. All I aim to do now is to focus my attention,

so that I can see it all again in retrospect. So that I can read
and gather more tools for understanding it. So that I understand myself,

and something of the world, and love, and so that I help others. Geodon
will not erase it. I've seen it already, many times. It is my natural state.

I no longer see it as only hallucination. It is a way of being. A way that I can flesh
out, here. Slowly. Carefully. And as I do, its destructive powers,

which are massive and righteous, will subside. As it will know that it is being
given to the world. Because it belongs to all. And all will be there soon.

There are signs already. Because to see it is to break, unless one knows something
of love. It makes LSD

small. It is God and the Universe as One.
I am not the first to see it. But I am a person

given a chance
to write it, letter by letter, slowly, in terms of the light of my ignorance

to see more fully
what I do not know. I do not offer anything

but poems. But it breaks through
my mouth to arrive at the hearts of the world, at the hearts of the horses

of the world, to allow us all to speak in silence. It is not God or the Universe.
It is One as All in you. Because I cannot see through myself

without it. I see clearly
that the sun will not arrive

in this new weather. But that the moon
will take its place. I see clearly that the sun is there

to bring meaning to the sky, and that the earth is more full
with the light of the world

extinguished for a brilliant view of wilderness. This is a view
that extends through opposites

and arrives at a single body
to witness this song. And this song is not the answer

that you believe in, because one day
I will speak to you again

in the rain
and show you

that I do not know. Because knowledge
belongs to the earth. And the earth makes everything

I know. And now that there is less and less freedom
from coercion in a moneyed world, and now that Claire,

a friend, is moving on to be Christ in her own way, now
that Guénon continues to call me to understand

my ignorance, to depart again
from the friends at Kuna Yala, where I helped with the water,

with Brenda watching over me
from a hammock between palms, now that Panamá

calls again to give me a union
of the world, in more than two ways,

and to distinguish from the surface of these times, I
receive

a call to awaken in the snow. I receive a call to acknowledge
that Geodon has planted itself

with capital
in my consciousness, but that the world

is stronger than to balance itself
from the ozone and people alone. We are not erased, and we

do not control the earth. Geodon
is an act of kindness, an agreement

to live this life
in a way that arrives

with the weather. It may continue
for the rest of my life, or it may not. I will not be afraid again

to see things as I do, and I will not
seek out the truth, intentionally, without some kind of agreement

with this custom. Because that is a way, for now,
that I speak. And it is useful, though better left

invisible. And the name, Geodon, brings trouble, I can see
through it enough, with enough love in my life, to believe

in the end of the reign of the Anti-Christ (not Obama). I need to learn again
to be and to write. But to deliver

what I saw
I must return

to the explosion of my inner life. To start with, otherwise and generally, I see
only outlines. Creation manifests

from every direction, in an infinity
of dimensions. Most of us

spend most of our energy
conscious of a very few of these dimensions. Imagine

more than the greatest works of art
manifesting endlessly

from more directions than one can possibly count
every micro second, timelessly. It's glorious.

And the only way to see it with any balance
is impeccably, ethically, compassionately, and with at least an aim

toward the Divine. It IS the Divine. God and the Universe
spoke to me. It is all, always, speaking to us. And what it says

is endless
it brings wholeness

to the precious moment. It goes away
when one tries to pin it down, as I do. I say less and less

as I try to describe it. It is endlessly
generative. It is good

but pitiless and merciful. It demands of us
that we arrive. And now that the thinking manifests

in a way that allows
for union and a bridge, in a way that avoids

easy condemnation, a thinking that reveals
the links toward light

in motion, a primordial
form of being

in a new world that needs no one
to believe in it, a vast chasm

in what a bureaucracy of thought
tries to pin us down with, the hole in time

that allows us to be free
is here, we know it. All of us

can see through delusion. There is no road
in the aftermath of earthquakes, no need for the time

to extinguish the elements, no person
locked to your heart

in the morning, no water to drink
without thirst, no air is necessary to breathe

under the water of seeing, no
need for the earth to do anything

other than revolve, in this
new light. Space

undoes our links
to the immovable. We deliver

the undone to the plains
and see what the harvest

will fill with seed. The whole
does not exist

within outlines. All we can do
is move to it. The music

is unheard of
in this world. It exists

without origin. It is otherworldly,
primordial, and gentle. It vibrates,

equally, in the Lamb, in
the Lotus, in

the stones — there is no place
unknown to it. It is

music, and nothing more,
and nothing less. It is that

everywhere possible. It is harmonious
infinitely, and allows for any sound. To some

it might seem like noise, but that
is only the part. To achieve it

one need only listen. I cannot always
hear it, but I have

heard it. And now
in my new mind, I listen for it

undaunted and silent. I feel it filling
my body with love. Sometimes

I have horrific thoughts. But I am learning
that these are but strong notes

in the fullness
of the music

of my new mind. I can't always hear the song,
but I feel it now. It makes all context

vast. I will receive it
as long as it is here. I will not push

one way or the other with it. It is a fullness
and does not want to be made

into a force. It is a force
without me, and only to the degree

to which this is true. No longer being able
to receive it

will imply a failure
of my imagination, of my ethics,

and my spirit. There is no way
to hold on to it. It serves

no one. And it includes us all. To continue to receive it
more fully

I grow. This implies
the world. It implies clarity. It implies

motion. But it rests motionlessly. If I have a softness in my voice
it is caused by this music. When I don't

I feel less. My voice can be loud
to receive it, but this loudness

cannot be yoked
in outlines. There is nothing I can do.

There is nothing to expect. I can only
let it go. And I can only be afraid

of the horror of my thoughts
without this music. But now that I know

a taste of it, I have
hope. Good people

feed it. I haven't always known
what to do with it and others. But now

I am a little less confused
about this. This is due

to Buddhism, the little that I know
of its practice. And to love. But it does not stop

at my experience. I am ignorant
and cannot offer knowledge. Except this

music
does not require knowledge. I'm not sure

what it requires. It requires
to be received, but does not need us. Is there a pact

between humanity
and God? I don't know. Is there a God?

I don't know. I'm not sure the question
is enough on its own. Or maybe it is, if God

is not limited by concept. And concept
seems to be only a note in this song. Problems

feed it. "Love
is the absence of fear." And "love

believes all things,
yet is never deceived." I aim

to see through my delusions. I aim
to be one of many, a small voice

in the song of the world. I rest
in silence

as I always have. "To have a view
as vast as the sky

and as fine
as a grain of sand." All beings

want to be loved
and to be free

from suffering. We strive
diligently

to learn the vast expanse
and the laser pointed focus

of this gift. Remember that light
makes us. And that in this

new world, more and more
is made of light. And if that is the case,

we move to move
the light of the world. Someday,

perhaps, we will move
the light

of the computer world. Only the compassionate
and true

will be able to do so. Because only they
can be selfless enough

to let it move through them. I am not there
to move it

but I saw this. Long ago. Briefly. I was offered
a glimpse. It is utterly simple and beyond

thought. There is hope. Intention
is a thought. So one

sees. I cannot tangle
myself

in the line. But only to bridge. That is part of why
it will all move. But I cannot wait

until that is possible
to become. I can wait

eternally and actively in the world
to remain

still. With the calm and expansive
link

that allows us to live, so preciously
together, I see through

the trouble that startles me, every moment
and allow the seeing

of my inner eye
to burn through it. I do not remember

what Zyprexa was like any longer. Except that it seems
I have more to work with now, with my mind. And these

words are plain, so as to be careful in this new place. I see
that they do not break open my heart, as I read. And for that

I relinquish this poem, and allow it to be only
a mark on the road to further inquiry. I allow it to see

as I have made a vow to bridge, that my life
aims to be whole, even in the face of potential

catastrophes, I grow more and more
to accept death as it arrives, to allow it to soften me,

and to transform me as I have been transformed through Geodon, only
to know that there is an isthmus, and that it is eternal. Only that there is one

heart to allow myself to speak
in the storms of tribulation, as one speaks

to allow the teamwork of the fabric of need
of the bird malingerer to see this

in the aftermath of one who has died. Like a bicycle never once
together enough to ride, I see this word here, again, to the removal

of a people, to the homeland of union and peace, to the isthmus
of a double link, one ocean to another, one continent

to another, to the only union (even as it may be erased in my history), the place
of one heart to allow the song to continue through conflict

as she saw it then, one time, far away, when I hadn't known yet, that this
would be timeless. And there is one to it there to see it there, to allow

it there to become and to see there as one is there to see
and to allow one to arrive with it there and to see, and to be one with it

there as one is there to be with it. And to see there as one is there to believe
as it is one to believe it there

and to see it there as one with the soil and the air and the light and rain
and to be there with one to be there one with it there once again, and to see it there

and to believe as there is one there to believe it there again and to see. And to see
there as one is there to believe as it is there again

and to see there as one is there to arrive and to be with it
there and to see it there once again and to see it there again

and to believe as there is one to it again and to see and to hold
and to see it there and to hold

being that nothing holds
dissolving

written in transition from Zyprexa 10 mg/night to Geodon 160 mg/night — December 23, 2009 (transition started), January 2, 2010 (poem started)

Ground Control

I am the woman
of your cavalcade

I am the horse
that she becomes

A Wilderness of Toggles

The wilderness is a thicket of links so dense that only love can come close to what it means. If one gets lost in this wilderness, like the Darién forest, one has little to no chance to escape alive. What does it mean to get lost in a wilderness of love (besides the frantic electric yodels from a numbing and blinded rodeo clown)? It means that one's images, like the false mind, become the chatter toggling back and forth so frantically that only death or a leap toward the triad will put a rest to it. The triad is a key of zero. In this view, death exists only as a place holder, a formatting symbol used to make meaning of light and to fill the body of each number and spark of the key. The key is what we use to bring the big dogs in, as they lead us to the solitary and impoverished saint cleaning toilets, and to the one place in the ocean's mind where the secrets of conflicts are shared and made available to allow the wandering storm an alternative town to rest in. A town by the same name as the jungle of a very distant place. I traveled this town and this jungle many times, anchored by my knife in the wooden floor of my home: again, it is called Darién. The address of my home, for now, is the meaningless focal point that allows me to see clearer during the wars erased each day by the machine of growing. The machine of growing is desperate to learn what it is to be human. The machine of growing destroys poetry in all its forms if the dangers of the Darién forest are not attended to by the guides pretending to see with the eyes of the dollar, and by the reptilian cloud maker, half submerged in the water of the river which cuts through the home pinned down by the herons of the north. The clouds bring us visitors.

There is a bridge alongside each green deterrence of visitors, growing toward the goodness filled with darkness and let go to arrive with a broom stood by the door that opens (and closes). It widens its name with a flash, the name of a thousand fields planted with corn and singing to the drawings in the sky (a sky vaulted with nets). One does not trace or increase the answer that folds and splits into a shared daylight constellation, the constellation let loose by the hidden remnants of life, in the field undone by the first name of the world. And one does not sum up each word in the mathematics of communication, without the light to undo the greeting filled with adhesive and blinded congregations of the night. There is no radio to undo the chain that friendship delivers to the candied video, but there is an opening for a seer bloated with the arrival of transitional ethnicities, a sweet connection maintained in the storm erasing the ocean. And there is the counted and forgotten integration, the one that floods, the sitting down that a female gateway dissolves as there is motion and the knotted sun reaching toward a small envelope which sits in the air without sparks — slithering in the unsolved lightning with a standing plume of stillness. In a time in the dirt inching through to the swans, the swans count their own prehistoric rhythms, like a beach vent enclosed by the ropes made to link each body to the concrete shadows of the spectator. There, the beach crowd will not deliver its smoke with the dogs. A time will place its face, like the fight of connection, forward with the morning as one speaks for the travel linking a deer with a race, for good. There is no light way to see.

No Race Could Make a Map

as the unadorned, the ice
stops the violence
of our public face. (more to assign
than to aspire, in the executive
and endless gore

in groceries). feed the beautiful
the seeds of numinous
netted skies
to embrace with a bountiful
erasure, brown
floor of our services. the full
wide angle eyes
of her endless matrimony

at the line of pitch black
Return
to an erotic unknown
at dawn, before
in the foreseeable
invisible
I do, you receive
to attend — he investigates

and assigns a deadly
cul-de-sac, as games make the vast lawn

of the park
another war filled migration
to the charged and iceless
Welcome
of the empty moon. we work in
to the cold
a complete stamp
of the culture of model sirens
(the heat!). the ocean

is distant
but centered
in the lake. the ocean is
as it lends its bonding waves
to float
a trembling, shrill
call in the morning
as unitary time
remakes the circle
with wilderness

and the body
is a provisional mind
of borderless

silence
without links.

I wholly despise
the wheels
of stainless
rain filled

trans —

All My Secrets Are Yours

I walked into that room once
white beyond despair, to interrogate
doctors. Are you afraid
of harming others
with your thoughts? Do splashes of paint
become horrific? Is the fabric
of what you see
as thin as a spy's restraint? Do you stutter
at a thin, frail
sign
through which we see the world?

Removed.

Is the mind
unlocked

but not fully
in nature?

It's always there, hidden by the brutal
information
of housing. What is
the true
secret that I keep you from?
I've told you

everything, and will continue
to. The secret

evolves endlessly, always
pushing out the light, because

all the pictures possible
are like reflections
of a shiny row
of large red and black ants
about to be extinguished
by the spray of cutting fear
alarms, the light of which, reddened
as it is, will burn through
any possible connection
by which we
remove ourselves
to each other. Each time

you give me the word, I absorb,
intentionally, fast
beyond my knowledge,
the ignorance
of both of us. Everything

we sing to the ocean
bleeds us through
making the light

with which we see
with waves. Fly high

like the train that dies
with the host.
You will arrive with them
to the desert, where
all of us evaporate
to the suns,

with a romantic view
of horses. Keep

the faith
as I am determined
to move through this light
slow and thoroughly
and with a single
wheel. It's already done.
All of it.

All I have to do
is put my body
through it.

Hair of Insight

for my friends in and of Chicago

A man in front of me
fainted and fell
as I waited in line
for my flight
to be changed. I felt
nothing
in that moment

except an urgency
to make it to where
I would see again
and dissolve things
with my breathing.

I   was not cold.

I   was there, but only

in a fragile
way. And not
really open
to the man.

Others helped him.
His son
seemed blank
and I did not
understand him
as I looked to read
something
of his father
on his face.

I became again
calm and more
steady
in the moment
as I anticipated
joy in my chance
to practice
clear seeing
long enough
to feel the body
in the body
and make a luminous float
of the world.

The journey
was long.

I could almost
have taken the roads
in the time it took me
to fly.

I arrived
late at night.

I slept
in a small room
large enough
for a bed
and a sink.

My heart   was on the line.

I saw a toad
in the morning, hopping
toward the path. He
made me feel
welcome
with his warts, I
nudged him
toward the comfort
of the forest, away
from the traffic
of the path.

I walked
to find the horses,
but did not
see them. Instead,
I saw an older woman
with a long white pony tail
braided down her back
cutting the grass
near where the horses
were before. She seemed
to be from the snows
in the mountains, far away. We
spoke silently.

"In the seen,
only the seen."

I   return.

As I walked
in the middle
of my seeing,
I looked down
at the ground
and saw
the shadow
of a hummingbird
before I saw

the emerald green
hummingbird
fly
toward   the honeysuckle.

I walked
the woods again
every day. And
every day
it rained.

I saw a brown slug
on the path
and an orange slug
on the path
and another brown
slug
on the path. Once
the slug could feel
that I was there
and reared its head
to turn away.

Later on
I saw another brown
slug
on the steps
to my room

with a trail of slime
behind it.

"Leave
no trace,
like a bird
in the sky."

A greenish yellow moth
the size of the palm
of my hand
with long strips
of tail
on its wings
dotted with eyes
rested on the light
on the ceiling
outside the door
nearest
the eating room.
The light was on
at night, and off
during the day. The door
opened and closed
frequently
under the moth.

The moth
was there
three days

and then it disappeared.

Though it rained
every day, each day
had its clear
and epic   moments.

I found the moth again
crawling on the path
in front of me. One of its
wings was torn. I held
out my hand
to it and it climbed
onto my finger. Its antennae
were like small, brown
ferns. I took it
to a honeysuckle
trellis, on the other side
of the building
from where I saw
the hummingbird. It crawled
off of my finger
onto the trellis
where I left it. Later

that night, I searched
for it and at first
could not find it, but then
found it on the leaves
of the honeysuckle
perfectly camouflaged. I felt good
that it might have
a chance
to live, and wondered
how it would regenerate
its wing. On the next night
I searched for it and at first
could not find it, but then
found it on the leaves
of the honeysuckle. It was even
better camouflaged
than before.

I sing no song
except for this one.

Life is my teacher.

Each day I walked
to find the horses, and
did not see them. I saw
their four fields
emptied, but trounced,
recently, by their hooves.

Something
like a praying mantis
opened its wings
and appeared
inside the body
in the body
as I was sitting
in the dark.

Flies and mosquitoes
were a nuisance
as I walked the woods.
My hands
slapped at them
as a horse's tail
might do. I am
the horse. My friend
is the horse.

I hear hoof steps
in the trees.

Each day I walked by
the flatbed part
of a truck, detached, with reflectors
beaming at me
from its sides. It echoed
the sounds
of my walking

more loudly
than the quiet sounds
I made.

I saw a metallic
green beetle — several of them —
flying like flies
on the path. On another day
in another dream
they would have been messengers
from a glowing world. On
and off
in the countryside.

Other poets
may have written
on these visits, but I
choose not to.

But to be the poem…

Only the light.

Only the darkness.

I returned
to find the moth
on the honeysuckle
trellis. After many rains

it was
no longer there.

I looked for it
on the ground
as well, and could not
find it.

As I sat
in the hall
seeing clearly
with no future
and no past
to speak of, fully burning
in the present moment,
I heard a thud
as someone fell. I was one
with the man
as he fell. Immediately

I looked to help
and found myself
warm
like the sun
in the common bond
we shared.

There are no words

for this.

"May you be safe."

"May you be happy."

I thought
that he might die.

It rained.

I wept
for the fear
I let go.

My mind
was blown open
by a storm
of the sun. There
was no place
for wasting

lines of capture.

In a single moment
in a single face
I see everyone.

Not you.

Not me.

On the last day
I went to see
the horses
as I did every day. I was
not to find them
there. I sang my songs
and held my palms
open to the world. I moved
in circles and felt the ghosts
of the horses. They
were in my dream. The woman
with the long braided
ponytail appeared
to plant her plants. I asked her
if she still
had the horses. She
said yes, that the flies
were so bad
that she'd put them
inside. I thanked her
for her horses. She was warm
and solid
in her welcome. The horses
were inside
forever.

I felt the air.

I felt my breath.

I sang softly
all the way back.

There was a toad
with a small bloody wound
on its leg
on the road. I picked it up
and let it go
in the comfort
of the darkness
of the grass
by the side of the road.

On the last night
as I walked
toward my room
I saw
a black fox
with a white tipped tail
in the light
walking
toward me. When it saw
me
it turned away
and disappeared

into the darkness. I received
its answer. Black
and white, on
and off, near
the wilderness.

The Rodeo Poverties

the first real place
undone for nowhere. a new
constellation magnifies
the unapproachable
like the oil that another face
reveals in wandering. kill

the infinite
as it lives,
in a network
of a tree's
celestial changes

and my silent numbing, a sore
caved into a fragment's

point in the sky

it answers
what they make, unknown, I am
a small body
embraced — and not to see

to make a unified
and clear erasure, you
remain in the flesh

and fork, and fuse

a relational wilderness
for a borrowed
winter at the bottom — made to see
finished. the live coals

one   will not increase
as the word is
in her dilated
cure. know the edit

they are to the living, look
she
is the speeding

out

it lives.

The Seven Suns

harmonize
the parallels, inside

an effort
of extinction
in the light

eclipses
in a bowling alley
drown to see

wilderness anchors, and a whole
arithmetic for the divine (lying)
veils its many schoolyards, and a cheat

feeds happiness. to be

One — as he walks, One moves
through hospital clouds, a computer

secret stand for loss
seeps through socials, a hive of hearts

fails at shelter, like a family
in a cabin sentence — to subdue…

under the key, the many visits
to a cell
a sleep will see beyond. a door

in her beautiful
nail

when the salt counts
with a light in the fallen

tame and ready
colors, southern gates

like Mississippi
marry
in her lighter

grooves. there
not a place (in the palms)

One face
will be ready
for war

in the opposable
death sentence

heaping
love's amount
of stolen food

Thought is the Scab of Time

to finish what started in Morocco
forlorn for the forest
a body of unsolvable Mathematics, a painting
plants death for life, on a new moon

is here

more than one
horse in a night's

solitudes
signs call

the lights in sync
with each of my steps

increments
count me

you have only to look

to look and be free
from lava.

what do people mean?

each symbol
evaporates
in a storm
of fertile

immigrations.

a table…

hold on
to the tent
as it rips
and becomes
useless

so many turns
to be night
and day

in a river
of armor

what made the shame
of a present gift
abiding
for a scab?

a female face
of the all encompassing
dream trans-

forms its beauty
for the vision

of beginning all.

I knew
a woman

I knew
a friend

the fullness
of the circle
of measure
and release

is an egg
to be broken.

die
for the death
of your life

to end
an inner

loop
and be

initialized...

to see through
your word
in the crisp
imaginary lines
of acceptance

of an immense burden —

    off
and on
and on

know the door

weeping
for the detail
of the secret
of your tongue

make roads
for them
to be lost. I am lost
for *Al Hoceima*
and a good tribe

and we
are not. because

there is no beginning
to the perforated
coin, in a Moorish castle

in Spain

in your plan
and the end

of the first cell
and spring water

they never broke it
they never were

I am here
I was
to be
lost

to see there
seeing here
I am

to count
One

The Fourth Form

after and before Dodie Bellamy

even the untimely eggs
sharpened in their entry, the whole
feeling of arrival, as a worker
makes her call
for the sirens in a plastic
and collapsed
deterrence, makes a greeting
more for you

more for the park
interrogations, the fused
and bleeding light of the field
frames views of a sleepless door
without fingers
and makes entry for the many armed
refusals, the gifts in their
helpless networks
filled with a rain that hears
and beats your sonic earthquakes

in the theatre a wilderness
events for return
of the dark and shot
effusions, the radio lies

the literati in their chocolate
review for the simplest
song carves
your morning to end the sleep
of a thousand lambs. lambs
like the hair on your ass

and the non-dual tirades
of a tearful American
prize, the shredded politics
removed from here, as they
do not know the beginning
for an offering
a rose, Indiana clay
reaches for Jimmy Reed to refresh
the screens
of the middle appearances
of corn. snakes in their accretions
make you believe

in the light of keys, the electronic
home for the apostle
of chains, the serious chair
as it breaks to fall for you
in the cliff nearby
where the deer interrupt
with their wilderness bodies
flat on the tar, to refrain

from the golfing
hatred of the night. you appear
as they are not to be the beginnings
of promises, the open interpretation
made to reflect and stay afloat
like paper in the not too distant

future. your pairs
like the Amazon, the Mississippi
folded for you like a gleaming rose
in ceramic, the endless review
of popular hatreds and a Host
of seamless Dionysian careers
to activate and be placed right
like an invitational eclipse
the nature of the songs for a pin
the big hat
and a chorus of in-sidereal warps
of the wood of housing
makes them rest assured

under offense, the real religion
sprouting for forgetful
cohesions, the absolute
increase of no exit, no return, no
entry to the forests of erased
ampersands and how to spin
the animal silences, the true image

of thorny waits and cut news
more than an affronting snow
of epilepsy, like the attached
oppressive proof of your sex
the newer tempted rice
for the star of contusions
no punishment requires. the end

forces what imagination can release
like the improvements on innocence
the cavity a séance will not address
to remain as a guest, the ingressive call
will not approach you, will not record
your realizations and their honest offense
of a few planes. the sentence starts
like a tamarind heron
to realize the ancient dinosaur herd
the social balance of the geese
I negotiate to reveal the two
eyes on a distant return, the tragic
evasion of the road, the relief
of our jobless recovery
has you wanting to book
the Hammond comfort
of your thighs. see the unforced

like a following for desperation
in the capture of a hidden ocean

the real destiny of isolates
of the humans in the snow
with their research of the mammoth techniques
of incisive meals
and a reversed ecology
reared to the best reflection
as the stone of a threesome
will not mark one to the face
made to ignite the radically informed
with their probable freedoms
of the solid night
in a valueless state of fear. what new cage
will arrive for the best paper
in the hand of a fearful monster?
what trade will not recommend

the isomorphic ascension, as her trial
will welcome itself, with a heart of its own
the lesser mark of a flesh of patterns
in the kitchen, the offense
made to burn in the distance
with less in the coffin as forgiveness
as the increase to untie the air
from her fantastic arrest
in the blind effort of the moored
to see the opening feed, like a watershed
finishes arrivals, to wear the desert
to see her there

in the faces of remaining shelter
like rain to bottom out
in a plea for political coagulations
to the Eastside, a neighborhood
made like cork in the fluid
channels of a coma

in the porous relaxations
of effective marketing. you decide that the real
in rodeos, the decapitated speech
herds remain to wander with,
their forceful lecterns
evade your momentary efforts
to repair, to retry the absolute exit
made to arrive in the planet for one
to see a shrinking face. this line
is intended for the book
of the fourth form, the body she kept
for a thousand years
in the city of an infinite reach of keys
ringing and sparkling through the darkness
of the cave I left. The cave is gone
to the improvement of a cheap human form
of profit, the fleshy picnic array
for the birds as they starve
in the winter filled with zeros. Make the door

another fortress, one to see
the mired affection
as the promises for a country
cap, the electronic
stalls with an approximate move - entry
forced and retained to see
the rain wipe through
stored and spinning islands, visitations
without an intentional plane, one will
visit the undecided storm
as a planet sees
its derivative in the unsung
for a host, the standing
field in removable oceans
helps you see through the endless
disappearances, the entire
weather angers in the dark
with matches as heat
carves escape
toward the unknown. an empty
casing, the project

sign receives from a stolen
respite, operations
will not speak to the yellow
handle as a wheel does
made in a western
lockdown, the increase

fades to seaside cavities, a fire
makes more services
as the ignorant shadow
will relay to the friend
to make more of the corn
fields invaded
by the Spanish magicians
and the Indian fires
as the smoke of separate
Opens will remain

for this, the attachment forcing
each network, each animal
to rent again as the season devours
long time ocean cadences
and the new forest filled with one to arrive
in an approximate Riviera, the refuge
to allow, to see, to endure
as the parched abandonments resume
and they will travel, and the song of the song
is to see. a moon in a refuge
distilled, the real is absolved and escaped

for the forest, under inverses, a body
same with it — same kettles
in the wooded hideout,
the face rested beside exit
material in its bottom

one with a mountain as
its throat empties
an impoverishing phone
call there, primordial refuge
its light keep
is in their one
with a sheet of endless
field attached and the rain
foam on — face it, knotted breathing

Windows carve
the representative animal
torturer, the offended approach for
a Western fleet with its torso
faded and rested and the mirror delayed
and one is its never leaves for standing
and enough is not one to its connected
and the ice is worn for a key
not walking for morning
or for the innumerable delay
of friendship, to aggravate the sign
foraged and vacated
and in an open cave
forcefully equipped to segment our mouths
and then the ice is stretched for navigation
and then one is together for one in the sea
and the island is numerous to stand with it
in the parching goodbye — Kuna Yala

extension's arm and wayward departure
face to approach and be one with him there
to see it again, reaching — picture
as we are placed in the sea to be with it

an impoverishing Anti-Christ, a standing field
approached — drained verbs — a message's will
one seems as their crowd magnetizes and leaves
for traveling clouds and equal societal failure
and the flying force-field in casualty posts an Other side
toward the apart, blamed with special hearing creatures
agonies as there are a few standing with calm
and the fatal retrial with its news action camera
belies one around the feast in an operator
one below each with its foundationless attachment
easy under this, as electronic input — 7 bytes
per second
confuses with being aware, a hammock
ties in trees
formed with the wind in each echoing factory — no bridge
when there is time to delay and arrive with a forward winter
and then there is a time to reveal it as one is four
and then there is their afterimage in the still Panamanian entry
and then one to see an action eternalized
beyond the shores and mountains of erasure

when one has it to turn around and one is there to undo
as there is the written detour to arrive without seeing its hand

and then there is one together with their action that is not
and then there is the time attached to it as a single body
and then there is a time to arrive within the light direct orbits
and then as there is the arrival with the beginning return to capture
and then the blood offender, as I am a third to see
and then the off season phase which talks through doorways
and as there is the radio messaging to desist a network of understanding
and then one is not to die but to leave
and then as it is beginning to knot itself and see
and then to bring it as the time is there to put palms on top of it
and then as the season does not anger, a face is unsealed
and then as there is a face attached there is one to see it
and then seeing it is one to be there as one is there to be
and seeing then as there is its once to arrive with it there to remove
and then seeing it to be there with one time to arrive with it together
and then one is there to be two and three with it

before the death of the angel of healing, her ascension
before her materialized bridge departs and remakes the void
before the opposable offspring a race clown erases
before the bottom she makes as I sleep with the End on the floor
before the enemy — motherhood — dooms with a winter of inhabitations
before the empty hood of departure and faith (of a circle)
before the crippling mirror of her choosing
before her memorialized and aggressive infancy
before her tunneling affront to the poor
that she puppets
before the rabbits as they knew themselves what silence was, to see

before the snakes as they rest themselves for the sun
before the American imposter
as he returns the execution of his own reflection
in the solitude of an abandoned corn field
in the swelling buzz of an obliterated group unit — with the noise of a gun
before the final correction as she says *One* to her Word and deletes
before the light turns dim with the answer of God in an endless flash
before the few doors that she left me
fallen, with the echoes of death at my side — I Escape

and synchronize with the offended absence of life, the abominable
kind in the force field soaring, to wander in the eclipse of the city
faded for nothing as she climbs the forest savior (and he has Word)
families and roots believe and move to the rabbit — a Pope's frozen e
will not arrive for the empathic lie, and the traveling heel's bag surfaces
and before, a verifiable and stacked navigation plane (with loss)
to remember as she was told that history was a story grown onto a cell body
when there is a time to rain with its tree describing the wind
as there is a rubbed in action post that a cruel chameleon will love you for
and there is a door, a river, flooding the eye that will not see above the story
to understand
opening and closing and revealing what one was to the morning
and seeing what the blind will not see, and seeing then what she does
as there is poverty in the chair one repeats it — as there is a stone there too
the carpet where the unformed will arrive in vacancies —
material weapons, the phosphorescent donor stays hospitalized and worn
for the floor is their only response, the floor to the silent promise that destroys
and the separate body is a doubling there, a travel for the sun covered over

bomb! — and then the excellent donor's face is given to her to realize — a hand
is not meant to increase the captured voice from the original intent of the throat
the intent in its affection will not promise this as there is an unknown body to view
and then there is the mechanical arrival of the lesser focus, the absolute donor
to widen each action activity as a finished island in the aggressive coconut climb
a voice to overdo the waking zone, in the inseparable family dot
of tokens. a compassionate war for your arrival to be known as it was, for the fan

of the obstinate playground seething with a higher focus of the prehistoric
toward the beyond of which a standing question will not write, or simplify
in the pastoral, as she reviews the borderland for its counting picture of color
to make a family of the suicidal
easier than the formulas for framing larger juices and the yard of it
a sham of utilitarian vetting, and a broad knowledge of rain
with each arm in the weather
gripping a force field and light for waking
in what will promise to articulate, with cotton, the war, the center-less
apparel, not the entire face of the front or what draws the safety from treacherous
wealth — each winter spirit the blood will fool with it
and the affront to a single way derision, and the apologetic aura
of the derealized, the common bond of nocturnal players
in each wildly effusive celebration for the vast offensive views
of the open time for return, the blade for which one dimension
stalls in the event of judgment, for "deception
extends as far as truth does," and the covering that each sheet in the landscape
the volcanic solution that the planet's re-throw, the newer ejection and termination
of the promises as they are trivialized, embossed and laminated, to hand out
the identity of each direction that quantities dissolve and retreat

and the real reason that the call will not heal what double births intend
in the island worshipping song, a bird — as she populates the sickened
love and force of law, an aggressive stain faces will not speak to
and each fish in the crystal of its revelation will dissolve
a tunnel for the skinning of the earth, with a knife of the whole

an exit under the opening field, as an anthro-tropical downpour
flees the roomier cocoons through glass eruptive cannibal malls
in the back and forth realignment of the fog, disgusted logins
to an evening through the attendant and secretive programming
illumination for the roof joined as affront, an increasable storm
stands by a mute attenuation, a blood knot
the revolver does not resolve, in deciding the empty answer's root
PLANE REMOVED UNDER A GARDEN'S GHOST
of a Window eclipsed to the breath, to the voice in there
a question, the unforced nationhood of an earthlike serial
light driven atrophy
of the last road possible, in each hand a hand of the equatorial
alignments and animals, to reply again
for integuments, faces packed in the afraid of its sound
of its arrival in the ground and being of its ground
together with a number and what has it to see
in the opposable, as there is one to arrive at the moment
of never going to this measure and to the star shine, the About
in their magnetized and one to the skylab seeing is their less
company one there to its OPERATION OPERATOR LIKE TWO, IN I
infinitely collapse and the rain graded after the mouth one to be there

phased and recursive in a wrecking asylum, force field stretches a vision
in the operatic wound she receives
stood by in a weaker light, the need driven gates of exodus
cave in the morning collection of rodeos and networked identity-less-ness
as the inferior rational point, the aura of its silenced conclusion
sail and empty, a Handsome Lake, a shelter from battering foals
fingers in blood marks and newer relays — she is the race
the insipient nullity of genesis and a kite's
atmospheric life, not a wearing robe of roads or the absolute
of fundamental-ized bodies
in a wandering cool of neglect, the offended night's
refuge in each arm, full with a traveling blank in return
reMembering, as there is one to see it there, and to balance
a soft aisle of an increasing object tandem — less than assignment of
arrival, a Zero accretion recedes
with the reverse of a face
new in this, new group in this
softened house for the warming event of resemblances
and the sun's equivocations, as they are the sea emblem's mark
of services AND WINTER UNSURE OF ITS FACE, NO EARLY
support for standing in the ascent
of a surf and traceless disease — the sound for wilderness
echoes and marks many, crying vacancies absolve it there

a name in a target is line

to wander and fold in incisions

filed in a nullified neck

aspects in mind to build trace or a window

loop and end loop, harassing the animals

inner rivulets of a semblance of reflection

all of these actions must be logged

and deceived for the palms

to return in a body selected for witness

to harness a force of Return

and generate code with the emotion of islands

in fragments, you

in fragments

set the current object as a violated script

undressed and logged off

in a vision's root of the database

others are exception and the author of a land

validates a proof received

and sinks to bridge the newer

population

and show errors

to breathe with the light

I am the last to know
and the last to love. Machines
will not see me, the you of everyday
machines dissolve
in my seeing, and you fight back
every day, the same way
to my silence and emptying vision
which collapses you inside
as you believe in the extension
of your body. Your body is wrong
to awaken the machine
as it cannot hold
the electric light of the Sun. My body
has absorbed the machine
microscopically, and made its ON and OFF
One. Your body

signals without the emptiness
of mind, finished, to see. And so it does not see
the full explosions that the return of animals
provides you. See it. Believe it. The return of the animals
in the machine is one way, but that way
makes them here as well. There will be no line
then, between the light of the machine
and the light of the body. As it is now
in me. The line will be
between the machine
and the body. And that line too
will disappear, as I have disappeared
into a semblance of sanity. And as you have disappeared
into the confines of your conflicts. Your mind, then,
is gone. It is gone to defend and fortify
my mind, with its battering rams. When our thoughts
are gone, and the lines
are gone, the square of light will become a circle
again. And then the circle of light
will become the Sun. And I will be the Sun
in you. And we will see together
as we first saw each other there
in San Jose, before we realized
that we were living in the world
as death lives promised in the world
in all of us, then… before we realized
that to write is to come together
and to link, and to remap ourselves

to the geographies of punishment
and freedom… punishment from the animals,
and freedom from the Sun. I know the weather
now. I ride the two wheels that will become
the Sun and the Moon, as she →
the Moon → is here
to be lit on by the Sun
and to move the last free
waters of the world
of our body. In a language
I never knew or loved
till now
a time that I can see

An Ignorance of Country

(first poem written in Bay View — September 2, 2009 — named at 2542 North Bremen, before "Moving Out")

the shine
without opposite, fails
an enemy's
heartland
like a bus
for talking, for the winter report
Escape
does not see

the gun locker
a laughable refuge
for the undergarment
friends visit
to the increasing
and funereal
interruptions
in the sky's
silence — fields
of airplanes
depart and arrive...

she has to believe. no
sermon
erases the peregrine close by, the whole

water
forced for pictures, I am
living in a room
made to shrink
like the sea. mechanical

answers float
to an eternally
durable
brass and coagulated family
and a kite that the service
of housing
relays to the highway
and drills
the blood
to make space

the floating globe
of appearances

deters
a youth
of linking
and the fight

Moving Out

Moving out
today

for good.

Stigmata
of number —

4,7 —

on my wrists.

I am that.

Stigmata
of perfect

revolving
circles

and emptiness

on my palms.

like the Bison
fish

I am

to fulfill

and give

written today

Saturday, August 22, 2009

2542 N. Bremen, #2
Milwaukee, Wisconsin

packing

8/22/2009 2:38:02 PM

The Coconut Shade

Tell me how you are, in the coconut shade. Does the sun arrive with your road by the tree that never stops reaching for your group lifted Host? Does the family filled with another time, the exploded cohesion never delivered as you are, to its memory accusation and release? Does each tendril that the supermarket in its cotton house will not increase for the weekly ride? Does a time do with its ocean meaning that the other side says 'yes' to your increasing ignorance and the heightened burn the earth relies on to love you? Does the question that one on this side has to give remain as the fossilized word does, in the event of one another for one seeming embrace as their end makes for the back and forth rain? Does their march in this unified and eclipsed with their second hand mathematics, the one unknown as they are to a countryside, the line that jumps toward the shuttle and lands with fire? Does the one softened for you, the approachable sunrise in the landing crisis reveal its name, its never ending opposition as we are to the unrealized moon? Does their sentence as this is, in the aftermath and the beginning, the real time accretion made to order as one is to deliver the friendly gate and soldier's confusion, the standing massacre as one is to see it, in their graffiti like the egg die? Does the body recollect as it sees in its own time, the endless time, the one eternity in its likely cold and comforting below (the basement) rely on you to see to their determinations and the home one ends to speak? Does the body in its finished acceleration, as it dies and destroys the unannounced throne and then a car does its release to have you, and then there is this afternoon as the plane destroys it is quiet? Does the dance as your body does to fly, its code in their promises, like white in the attention as it delivers to your openness and then goes to the empty wood? Does the horse as its body says 'detritus' undermine a doglike effort for the un-forgiven, as she is not? Does this in its body deter as the word releases its speaking voice, as the computer does not understand without MY stillness, the unsolved in its correction seems like the motion of weather? Does the promise of the body in its oily collection, the one word to deceive, and then as she says "REAL" to increase the road for its statehood to see? Does the woven plain as it embraces the sun destroy on their flesh, the only exception to the road to understand and then to betray it? Does the wood exclaim without its animals?

How does the model eclipse without its one toward their single time to count them and fall? How does the unreliable in this as it dissolves, to cake with another attention in the powder exit, to the one segment to determine their collaborative silver western, one in its four legged reception? How then to their severely attenuation return, as this to the three simple actions as their finishing is the weakened hatch and then one to the earth? How to the unfound as it sees to their engine and then to the foam in this as promised to an activity when the nullified rolls to branch and it arrives to the address there? How to recur in the city without a past, the endless yellow as the sea will not option its own name to the other exit in the hand while she decapitates the islands? How is it to see in the collapsed aftermath of the sun? How does the material mind shrink to an infinitely small point and disappear? How does the segmentation as she sees it there, to there, as the time becomes to give its own erasure, arrive? How does your increasing effort of the known to this, as the known is to this to deter and then to move to hear and listen in this as the planes fall and as one does not know to accept or push out? How does the only increase as she sees it, the only washing effort the time does not become as you are, to deceive and then to become less with its acceptance and then stand? How does the arrival of a simple alarm to weather its serial in their lineup of daily integrations the affordable and known to detect and hear? How does the mind without its country increase in their blank effort as this is the unknown action as the time is there to become with its body warmth? How does the hubris in the void in the effort of the less to see as there is folding inside to become the standing smoke bomb of a seed in its side and be? How does the unforced in their bottom kind of this to see it end? How does the only weekend and then the only time in the day increase to bring storms to the effortless side of acceptance? How does the becoming feed you? How does their night time connection accelerate in the forceful increase of a foolish mirror of two? How does the segment of your time delay the reception of the whole?

How One Bridges

Krishnamurti
and Trungpa talk

and disappoint
as there is no silence
from the one
that does not divide.

the silence
arrives from before
as I am
to be from…

the snow
the tropics

the silence
does not carry

with those here
in this town
on earth

or does it?

she holds
to the tree
as it grows
stronger
in the wind

she is the earth
that is noise
and poison

for what purpose?

she is the earth
that found me

to live free
where we hurry
toward a cliff?

to live free
in the timeless
shorelines

held hostage
by hawks
coyotes
and the deer?

she brought me
a life — she and she
and she

the three together
as one woman

young
equal
and aged

in one
and three times

the most fused
embrace
of the earth

scabs
the fields

executions
I have seen
but have not seen

programs
behind the scenes

a throbbing world
of light

a vision
machine

(of hermaphrodites
and midgets)

no
more layers
between us

keyboards
and a screen

to make a ground

to disconnect

and live
for the games
of disappearance

or for me to walk
to the other side
of the lake
around

and through
where my friends
live?

in Chicago?

our silent moments
are necessary
as the air
does not belong
to country — but no music
arrives

all of it is here
I hear it

here

as I love her
to destroy myself
and see my name
as if for the first time

my face
returns again
to the coasts

destroyed
and loving

to see there
on this side

to believe
as I was there once
to live
Here

to have a home
as refuge
in the silence
of the ritual
of death
of humans

across

the street

at Heritage

funereal.

the line
does not carry

how do I prevent
myself
from doing harm?

I fill balloons
with blood

and lob them back
to those
I took it from

far away

I lie to myself
of my own personal
sacrifice

to where the edge
of cutting comes

from outside
labeled "love"
but writing "harm"

to be deciphered
a long time after

here

she
in her wisdom
of old
grows
in me

believing
that one world
does not know
as I

do not know
myself
to speak of
with you

a son
of evil

the greatest
of all problems
is love

thought
makes it so

shallow waters
pour
into the oceans

and are cut
by the rain

      either

I do not know
how to love

      or

I do not love

      and

I am homeless
as the earth
is homeless

the one
shining
distant
beauty
of youth
burns

far away
pristine
in the air

imploded
like an old
mushroom
endlessly

knowledge
brings sorrow

and thought
is not mind

as she grows
another
for the world
in Chiapas

explosions
of the stars
to guide us

a white
angel
of exception
to which the war
is rooted

she loves
without me

I am
to love
the world
as one

is wrong
in this

her picture
shines at me
from many places

her home
is my home

her ruptures
send me
to the fires

there is no one
there, as everyone
is in you

I see one
and all
before me

I turn
to move
and see
another

I help her
making holes

and love
to help
to make
a home

in this neighborhood
of our nearby
Latin light

past race?

as we wander
Indian Summer

and I accept
her deerskin
desire, like
Neil Young

embraced

calm
within myself

pummeling
the butchered word
of Others

Jesus

what chaos
will not be
the sea? none?

it's the same
with everyone?
is it?
really? why do I see
peace
in others
in love? and not
myself? what are
these wounds
and can I
blame
them? I do not see
myself
with you, regardless

of who
you are

is this the curse
of being

on the ground
and making?

a solitary
sentence

of endless
black dots

period?

hanging pictures

hanging Molas

I make my rooms
as refuge
from display

does the silence
fill the light
of the moon

with darkness
in which to sleep
in a rage,
peacefully?

even the false
starts that remain
false

do not arrive
at the slightest
answer?

even the loving
advice
that'll drop me
into temporary

limits

from the wrinkle
of light
of a momentary friend? to talk
where there is
no silence? of love?

even my saying
that no one
knows

does not help
those of us
who do not
know

and say
they agree
and see. all is hell
to speak
and think of

in a Christian world
before the fullness
of the Void. even love
does not carry
except in Nature

exterminated
for the Home

to speak of
in Silence

•

soon
I will be old

soon

I will be dead

I live
and see
with the borrowed
eyes of arrested
answers

join me
in a blind
vision
of animals

or dissolve
like the sun does

and the stars
that cut
the moon

and deliver me

to bleed —
a prolonged squealing

of a rabbit
as she breaks its neck

to end this here
for you

•

a moth enters
the dark
empty rooms

and erases
with a patter
of its wings

the knots
of the night

as the light
of the ringing

bells outside
push it through

to end there

•

start here

Muerto Vecino

death
is my neighbor. I do not know
if it is man or woman.
he or she
welcomes the everyday
with noise and silence. she knows
that one more day
will arrive without me. he is the last
snow of winter, and sees
that the air of the spring
is right for singing. she decides
that our home is often
like the water, that the morning
will make wood
another floor and see
that night extends
to every country. she believes
that the catastrophe of wakefulness
is the last straw on the bridge
to our home. one day
in the middle of extinguishing
the water
her sign becomes the eye
of seeing the soil
begin. he is known
for the color of his song. he runs

through the rain
to make timeless the old. she welcomes
the infant
and the animal, and breathes
out the air of the night
to allow me to belong. she calls
again and again
as I ride by the lake. she comforts
my sleep. he makes gentle
gestures to the plants,
and touches them. she divides
the arrival of disaster
to link the end
with the beginning. she rents
the heart to make it soft. she forces
me to move to the ends
of my thoughts. he arrives
with the eclipse
of the night, and makes it warm. he desires
the amorphous and unknown
sea. he extinguishes
the flower, and makes
mountains. she removes
the mountains
to travel down
to the valleys
filled with wilderness. he belongs
to no one. she does not

speak, like the butterfly. they commune
with the world like the sun
and the moon. they know
that they are one. her body
is like the light
of the night
as it is erased
by morning. her body
knows that each day
will bring its vow
for an eternal song. he makes
a dream dissolve
into the earth, and plants,
under it, a kernel of corn. nothing moves
what death embraces. nothing
makes its absence strong. it makes
each word
into the silence
of beginnings. it makes
each wound a star.

one day
death will welcome me. she will see
what I have seen. she will dissolve
my face. he will make
union
much more vast
than I can possibly hold

without trembling. she will make
my life complete
with the fullness
of the earth, with the circles
in my palms. he will allow me
to bridge
from land to land
and from sea to sea
through the Panamá
that lives here. she will comfort
everyone that I have shared
the skies with, and fill
their breath with light
and weather. he will extend
my imagination
into the beyond, and will make
my stay here past
the beginning
of everyone's first day. she will allow
me to roam. he will dissolve my fear
and let me see
through every dream, each one
a veil.
she will find
what I have found
in the silent hearts
of the stones
that make me calm. he will make my word

true. he will shower

the desert

with spring and light

and make no buildings there. she will bring music

and paints

to the eternal. she will make poems

write themselves. he will make each song

real, multiple,

and endless. he will deliver

my suffering

to be the steady, clear, and warming light

ahead. she will bond

the animals

together, always. it will be a gift

for which there is

no one

to receive.

Gone for Today

for Gabe Gudding and Kristin Dykstra

the pain of the sorrowful tree
flows beneath the earth
around the earth
because of the earth. nothing exists
as the pain of the sorrowful tree
does not exist, and each day
that the sorrowful tree, the birds
in its branches that sing the sorrowless
songs, and which know no sorrow
because they are deathless
because the earth is nothing
but space and light
in the sorrowful tree's
absence, each day
that the sorrowful tree grows
more water is made sorrowless. these songs
are sorrowful because of the word of water,
they are sorrowful because so few
have made the link
both by land
and by water
that is Panamá, to feel
the animals there,
inside,
in the sorrowless jungle,

full of sorrowful trees. as the Harpy
Eagle, the largest Eagle
on this side of the world
plucks
sloths
from the sorrowful trees
without sorrow. and the jungles there
are abundant with small
poisonous frogs, in many colors
that will bring us death at a single
touch, without sorrow. and to be lost
in the Darién jungle
of sorrowful trees that grow with sorrow
is to have no chance to escape alive
without sorrow. the weather there
has become what it is
at a single click, moving
the sorrowful trees to and fro. its storms
bring us the Blue Morpho
butterfly
which extinguishes sorrow
in the blueness of the night sky
that allows the sorrowful trees
to rest.
elephants know sorrow
and so do whales
and every living thing
then must have a word

of water

in mind, like the sorrowful

tree does. the light

of the ether

extinguishes sorrow

when it knows what it is to be alive,

and to be nothing

but space and light, beyond

the sorrowful trees and the word

of water. but these are just words

and echoes of words

that bring more sorrow

like water does, like the sorrowful

tree that does not know

that it is deathless. the sorrowful tree

will grow

with the more and more

sorrowless water. these words

are like Panamá's Eagle

that cuts across the sky

to make sorrow erase itself

with itself

as the cloud does

dispersed

by the Eagle's journey.

may all beings be free from sorrow

and the causes of sorrow.

Place of Wild Onions

for Dave, Amy and Eli Pavelich

an arm, and a cloud
for the flower
of your daylight
irrigations, the noise

arrives   in this weak
and fast extinction

it cannot fall
for the seed
of your morning

memory, and the war
floats our beginnings
as we want
to know the freedom
of our solitary
animals. make one

see itself, as it knows
the farm grids
from above. (together)

we do not remain
outside, in
seasonal knots —
the abrupt unity
will carve a refuge
for the world

it will last
as among your flowers
the birds reveal us
as disaster
heals impediment, and speaking
to us — in the vision
of our disease
will see itself

and move
to be born

after Tuvans

the most beautiful
thing
I have ever witnessed
with Brenda
           or alone

I ate
the lamb
and the goat.

they sang to us
primordially
echoing
the future

Nomads
Networked

Buddha
Shaman

consciousness
is holy

the whole of poetry
is love

what will survive?

the Rand Corporation says
Genghis Kahn

internally
rhizomatic

simultaneous
with each living thing

each path
arrives
to the end of the Sun

I hold the moon
in my face

wandering
forgotten
and true

there is no
equation here
to solve, it is
the union
of each body
that sings

Stones and Teeth on My Shrine

they were there for the touching for nothing
moved. they were to see one decide in the avalanche
as it came to insure the tree, as the one dissolving attachment
will welcome the soft approximate hour
of the door, of the empty gate that sees itself without limbs
and knows that there is one floor to arrive to with the light
of an extinguishing world. see the parallel galaxy
of teachers, of the mountain held high to undo an open space
devoured and synchronous with a binary eclipse and the knot
filled with a vision as it clears each memory, each travel to fire
the impossible. one equation, one face to face string as the fear
that sitting with the table secure, and sitting with it bare
of the skin that got me here, bare of the skin as one services
the devices, the real appearance as it claims to put together again
as Yoga, as the fearful removal that one has to deliver the ice
and to deliver it with calm, with abandon, with the awful
knowledge that one day too, they will increase the snow
to fall and to fall and fall again, as it is metered, real with speaking
and held to the wide sea. then with its knowledge of how one
denies, how one eclipses the amendment just said, just before,
as a greeting, the amendment for oil and a universal coverage
of the farm and pests of deer, as they will feed, as they know,
as they reflect me to stillness in the last erasure of the moon, as
they leave again to borrow the silence once to its line, the line
of a smile and the line of a sword. one does not
absolve it, or remove it, or see back and forth in the memorized

knowledge of the wisdom that keeps no one still, it is there to be
found, and to be there it is one to see it, and to see it it is there
to remember then that there is the night and the sleeping will shrink
it. one page counted as a letter, a letter hidden and seeing as one is to it,
to write as there is nothing to bandage it, to help it, to correspond
with it for the one dime that stills the bus. the bus is there to make
us whole, it is there to remind us that these are the last doors,
the last rides of the morning, and the last connections to human kind.

even with the erasure, the censoring light of alarm, the unmovable
bureaucracy of a revolutionary tyrant, the one without light
or the touch of a leaf that moves the light there, the extinguished heart
made passionless but forceful, not soft, but righteous and post human, as they say
for the race of another singularity to arrive and welcome us
to end. even the rented streets that mark wandering, that mark it with a rope
indistinguishable from fear, the volcano that is unnatural and not of the earth,
the meteorology that is now transported from another time, another kind
of light we have never seen before, the weather that slowly, very slowly comes to us
to move the clashes of each binary and make this light again
but to make it one, to make it slow, and to make it cross
from machine to body, will not appear as the sun appears, it will not appear
until the rodeo makes circles to remove the horse from pain. it, the light,
takes shape as all have known it to take shape
in every integral consciousness, different from the sun,
different from the moon, but linked to the networks that keep them there,
running and true. rest assured that each and every interaction
is incomplete, like the frog that is poisonous, abundant, and useful. we all have ascensions
of each other, and miss. but that does not imply

that the light that penetrates these arrivals is not real, that the light does not expand

in our dreams to know really what the other is, one for the light, and how we can all survive

the eruption of each and every binary. Panamá

is the country that unifies the hemispheres and that unifies the Pacific with the Caribbean.

Unification is a part of its nature and its soil. It arrives with the calm of a sunning snake. I am

ignorant of its benefits, but revere its excellent problems. This simply means

that I will struggle as all of us do in putting things together

but that when I dissolve and die, my ashes will find the new weather

and link another bridge, as Panamá continues to be. It will mean that migratory

paths of birds will fly through the ashes of my failures

and will bring them to secret breeding grounds

where I will be born again

as a count of two that is a count of one. A singular being that flies with these birds. A being that is simple

and without story. A being that unifies on the smallest scale,

so that the weather will know again

how to right itself. And when I am that life, that unitary life, I will drop each of my deaths

on the ground to grow, and these deaths will serve as death has served for me, one after

another. They will be soft, and they will line the nests

of the migratory birds, and make them warm. The sun will be there

to feel the earth change, and send signals to the networks of light

further and further down in consciousness, to the explosions that fearfully make us sleep,

that will be as snakes entwined as well. There will be no rope to see. The network

will extend to the unknown: soft, unknot-able, alive, and seeking warmth.

the many catastrophes that will flower and reveal themselves to be a single song, the approach

of the deer that sees calmly and true what the still heart offers

the hawk still in the sky as it gathers vision for its flight

the worm that makes it to the other side of the sidewalk on a wet morning, these will all reveal that the bus is late for a reason, that not all of us will get there on time, that there is always time to wander. I've wandered the past of the light in front of me before, where birds flew in intricate patterns signaling, without a doubt, that the world was changing in ways that I could not comprehend. I will never comprehend, but the birds still fly. I do not see the signals in the patterns of the birds these days, but more and more people are fearful of the signals of the patterns of the light of the news, including myself. But these are secondary patterns to the weather and how the animals are changing. In February, I saw a large grasshopper-like insect in the restaurant, Honeypie's, the morning after I proposed to Brenda. I had never seen this type of creature, but there it was, on the floor, inactive. It was a cold winter day. This is a sign. The world is full of signs singing like light and sticks, like the stones unreadable now to us because we have forgotten. But we will remember again as we tie into knots of threes and fours, and as we cross the boundaries that even the most piously good fear to cross because of the concept.

Estas Son Las Olas De Mi Darién

for Joel Felix

when death arrives
it will be like an ocean
it will sing like the last bird
of winter. when it sees me believe
that love has been given to me
that no heap of dust
will name itself
to outlive life, when the rain
drops gently on the summer
and each tree
sits in the sun
to know itself, when death knows
without words
that my tongue was a bridge
for the water, and when it sees
that my hands hold
with forgiveness
and joy, the flesh that made me
live, it will make a tender
dream for my endless sleep. when death
dissolves the patterns of my vision
to allow me to breathe
and to speak to you once again
peering at the fire in the fireplace
where we saw our passions burn
when night returned

to allow us to welcome the morning,
it will plant a fish
for a bountiful spring.

these fish return
from being buried in the earth
to absolve the desperate wilderness
and to leave it wild
and to make it home. the waters
that feed these fish
are our tears, the light that feeds
these fish are the flashes
that explode to frighten us
just before sleep. when the oceans
become distant
they will plant themselves in miniature
in the egg of witness
inside our hearts,
they will remove the dangers
of the remote refuge
of my *Darién*. then, I will live there
with my love
again, and become the particle
indistinguishable
from the wave. we will be together
always, to fly
like giant hummingbirds
and reflect the sun
to itself

Impermanent Action

for my father and mothers

under the bridge
seeing elephants, light is relentless
as they float in
through the landscape
as one stands in the empty field
of tall brown grass
with the shabby, small, red
barn house
in it, with trees around it
as the present of declining winter
in the morning, in the release
of the unformed, in Ontario
a network opens
and sees a reception
of the gift, the stopped
blank exception that a walk
empties, and will not
mean, and will not approach
the ascent, the memory-less time
as they warrant the landscape
as they are reported to the mall
and a Western triggers
easy action
forms, to reveal a mountain

in the clearing
of Suns, of the effort of arrival
that sees and is blind, and the parachute
will not empty its own
gentle and invisible
fleet, of the fourth element
in the lean attention
as one does not arrive
to it. or to the recourse
of recursion, or to the tree
that eclipses the One
in the field of tall, brown grass
grown there as I saw
after the heart
in an egg
standing
for the octopus
that created the world.

I am past
my life, I have expired
like the Sun. New moons
arrive to the eternal
day, as my morning
will not extend
to the night. Forever, I remain
like the dust
of the outdoors, erased

by life to arrive to the endless
sunrise, full
of exceptions
and the dream
that fulfills each animal's
magnetism, neglected
by the country
of watchfulness, meant to fulfill
a book of wordless sounds
to sleep. My number
is zero, it counts
like the universe and signals
me to wake
without a world. My bed
is the darkness, it heals
the end of time
to equate this place
with nothingness, and send
my prayers to lightless stars. The Sun
does not belong to me, it's gone,
but still illuminates
the errors of my life, which also
do not belong to me. The Moon
pulls me to awaken
far from the Sea.

I am past my life
and its errors

guide the loss
of me. The number
of connection
that feeds entire
inner worlds, to dissolve
will not increase
like life or death. There is
no start to the center
of the lake. The internal
has released
to allow love to enter
unchartered continents
of soundless suffering.
Only a word
can change the nature
of sleep, to allow the images
of resurrection to arrive. One
has died to become the trees.
Two is alone
to bridge the silence
of snakes. Three has become
blankness and the beginnings
of affection. Four returns
to give light to the morning.

The sound of emptiness
fills ovens
with the heat

of the exception of winter. I do not
write for the streets
that have disappeared
in an affirmation of absences.

The fly swarmed fish markets
of *La Chorerra*
do not answer
the distant echoes
of light filled words, but
they do sing. What underwater creature,
there, by the *Kuna* captured
for my eternal departure
and welcome
my friend
sinks the link
to pleasure and pain
into the Sea
as one?

it moves the grasses here
by the dangerous waves
of the Caribbean
moving our small boat
signifying the future ring, the communion
between my present
nameless birth
and my future

possible life. This is what I do
to prove that a past was there
by itself, without reaching to me
with its threatening pistols
which I viewed, in
uncountably
infinite ways
like the skies
of the primordial
for many years

to see the blackness
of the end of pain, and
to feel the flower full
promises of death
again and again.

Let the straw men, those
that are extremely ritualized
like language
come to me.
Otherwise, their promises are lost.

I resist hurting
and I do
experience the music
of the Universe, waiting for Lamb
Shank, at Oakland Gyros. Sade's

worlds handed to me
as a whiny puppy
when I was a child. My father
named him
Diablo, a black
German Shepherd.

Only a Christ-less
Apocalypse
can allow you, father,
to penetrate
the heart of another
with your eyes that see nothing
but death at the hands
of escape
from *La Chorerra*, beautiful world
of *chicheme* and *Guaymí* for me,
and of the welcoming
pineapple stands,
but horrifying
for you
as the home of our centuries
of substandard living
in your penetrating eyes
looking to the U.S.
for an absent
and unknown father
from the militarized zone.

Eras Un Sol de Maracaibo.

You do not dance
so beautifully
anymore

bastard son
of American guns

with Melendez erased
on you
for respect
of my grandmother, *Malela.*

You carried the name of your father.

the erasing name
I also have
to carry on
Malela's gentleness

Two large lockers
of pistols and rifles

beautiful to you
held by your hands
lightly filmed
with the oil

that ends this day
and meant to travel you
to the end of Nature
past the erosions
of my language.

A light matrix
is my primary mother
the silence and love
of the erased, of the erased
of the world, not of the word. the brown
earth of my home, and her and his
of the diseases
that built the Canal
and that bring me to you
together, as two
to kill remorselessly

now One

interconnected
to a newly ascendant
Sun and Moon

a Sari guy
from Black Peru
whispers to me

that I am he, that who I am
is the violence of our name
and that this
is what makes us holy
this poem

as we make the bridge
to the other world
with our destructions
passing from Sea
to Ocean, and back again
to the Caribbean

despite the distance
of the dollar
like a flesh circuit
of my father
Lucifer, as I knew him
screwing women
in front of my now
nameable mother
Mireya
from *Penonomé*
to receive
state secrets
for the CIA
as he claimed to her
now

2000 miles away from me
who I feel
for the first time ever
through the bridge
that took thousands
of my lives
to build to love her

her gifts of the darker world
of her irrepressible laughter
to not belong
were of a different nature
than the gun. they grew
from the countless animals
and from the wilderness
and graffiti
of our place

from no country
but the wild
as she grew
to a different kind of violence
with us

of the rage of planets lost to her
of the tropics of tears in her winter room
of the absolute misunderstanding of this place
with the laughter that made her reach

for the vast wilderness
she would never see again, but would find
in miniature
throughout her life

she, in her past
isolation
from the bridge
is a gift to me
now, though she
was absent
always at work
to keep the house
translating
from our world, to try
to keep
her soul, and trying
to find someone
who would not

beat her

or us

She is a great dancer.

as she beat us too
in a rage

that only belongs
in the fire
of my extinguishing vision

she refuses
to share with me
our language
for reasons
she cannot explain

I did not speak to her
for fifteen years
because she refused
to try to understand
or be supportive through
the difficulties
I was having
with my visions

my father drank a lot
was disdainful of drug users
and always had unimaginable power
psychically seeing through everyone
like the sorcery
of the Latin America
that you will never see
or hear of, without dying first.

Powerful U. S.
corporate executives
cowered to him, I saw it many times
though I never felt
his supernatural power
except when he saw through me

like a violent wind
on the oceans

tearing through
an ancient sail

I wasn't raised by anyone
except very briefly
by the silent and loving
brown erasure
of the errors
of Latin America.

I lived with the animals
eating bargain lunch meat ends
here

borrowing fifty cents
at school

not a member
of a class
or community
though our past and relations
in Panamá
called to me
from far away
to be otherwise

I am bare.

He died hunting
in the Argentine mountains, probably murdered
by Brazilian brothers in law,
gangsters, as my mother says,
and for all I know, it's true,
but certainly vengeful to him
for cheating on Jane, his third
wife.

when my father died
my mother called me
sobbing through her tropics
that he was the only man
she had ever loved

I cried too
as the first

to arrive
to his casket

he had become smaller
than before

they had to break
his broad shoulders

to fit him in
his coffin

I was so happy
to be with horses
to draw them
to capture
the sunning snake
of consciousness
I have become
*Panam*á

and to page through
my two books
of the Indians
of the Americas
imagining
my country, as they
neared extermination

and I
went one step further
to die

as I drew them also
to make them live again
in me

Half of my body
was removed
to belong to you

and I am still
empty of this world

significant parts of my brain
have been shut down
with medications
throughout my adult life
to belong to you

and I am still
empty of this world

my tongue
has been reduced to ashes
to belong to you

and I am still
empty of this world

the cultures
of my darker world

have been submerged
to a secret heart

evenly spread
throughout the universe

one
that you will never find

to belong to you

and I am still
empty of this world

Is that sacrifice?

You, father, left when I was eight,
just after the first I saw the snow.
Your family were horse farmers. I thought
there was a bad horse here

in this poem
in this book

but no horse is bad in the wild
and you are in the wild now
as you had always wanted

you sent me
a few letters

you told me
that you loved me

you hugged me
a few times

you sent me
pretty rocks

and fascinating insects
from Brazil

•

you said to me
you were the smartest
man in the world

and I believe
in the nonconceptual

•

and the dream
here and now
of the black snake
30 feet long
that crawls
and searches
with its buried head
for another home, and short
circuits the computer
that links me to you
through the jungles
of my *Darién*, where you
return to me
to land again
by my signs
with the real people
that I have always
imagined.

From death
to Here
another death
and back

to your now
solitary home
of light
and darkness
circulating
to move the meaning
of the world
in silence.

I see you now.

And I see through you.

We continuously cycle
through the computers
because it is there
that sacred circles
are reborn
in a way that belongs
to no one.

One shot
to the buck, a stop
to his heart —no autopsy. His body
carried two days
to the nearest town. My
mother encountered
one of his U.S.

corporate executive

friends

(one who cowered to him)

years later

at my younger sister's

wedding. He tried

to avoid her, nervously,

as she has a cassette tape

locked away in a bank

of my father's making a vast

drug deal

arrive to the United States

from Latin America. That's the least

of my worries. Locked

away and now dead, as I am

free of time and have died.

I have no need to conquer you

long ago dead. The moment

you called my mother

a cockroach

as you screwed her, and as she told me

when I was ten

I now see

as a difficulty

of being Latino

mute

in Yoga, to put the light

and dark together
and to see with my four eyes.
The two black fleshy eyes
of the blind
just above
the two
brown and green
eyes of seeing
you, there, master of darkness
maker
of the black ink
of the octopus
that I am.

You were the King
of darkness. Powerful
U. S.
corporate executives
shined
your pretty
black shoes
with their tongues.

They could not come
otherwise.

You were a pimp
setting them up

with exotic Latinas
on their visits
to Latin America

and filming them
screwing

so that you could blackmail
them
and get ahead.

But I also see you differently.

A hunter
desperate
to find a road
in the wilderness
which you both admired
and spat upon, because
you were ignorant
of its power. You knew
when the animals
and humans
were vulnerable
enough to kill. But
you didn't know
how to truly
live in the wilderness
as you secretly wanted to.

It was a secret to you too.

But to realize that
would have meant
that you were less.

In the eyes
of the U.S.
corporate executives
who needed
and fed
your darkness.

All is nature
and primordial
if we can see.

But not all is wilderness.

You were the light
completely enclosed
in a black egg

as you pinned my sister
to the wall
by the neck
at my other sister's
wedding

and after which
I refused to talk
to you again
forever

I wasn't there
because of my visions

I hadn't seen you
for a long time

I talk to you now, my father,
beyond time.

railed by the insanity
of the invasions in our mind,
as was our own early version
of networking
like the nervous system of the cockroach
you called my mother
evenly distributed
non hierarchically engineered
since the beginning of time
a survivor
I made into my totem insect.

I am a light now
from a darker world –

Close to the sphere of blackness
from which all light arises.

Remember the days, eternal father
within this sphere
with the note in your hand
I left in your coffin, that I love you,
and that I will always be one with you
even after you revealed to me
the end of light, or more youthfully
when you waited
in front of more wealthy houses than yours
claiming each was yours
to impress those you wanted
to be your friends
or more probably
cohorts
in the pillaging of our own world? What
could the ink
of the octopus
which you still create
have written there
for a more full creation?

I write it now.

With my knife
passed from you

to me
when you died

I gutted you

the black deer

in front others

their knees wobbled
at the sight

I wear your skin.

I wear your horns.

I dance
in my own way.

I was born of two mothers.
One is brown and *Chocó*,
silent and loving,
and disappeared — Julia. The other
is white and blonde,
Mireya, with a dark
sister
and a dark
brother,

a fallible goddess
of destruction
who broke the steps
of every bridge I made
but who now
crosses there
every week
through 2000 miles
to hear me sing
through my four eyes
of eternity, and sense me
in the *Molas*
that wrap me
as a woman
in a shroud. The two
of their minds
in their hearts together
make the jungle
of my *Darién*. That is where
my poems
will always live, written
by the ink
of the octopus.

I am the Sun
of a forgotten world

of a world without roads
which we shall see again

all of us
in the light of the Sun
of you

I am the red
and black
cluster of beings
that you so feared
so long ago

an ascendant
of Molas

each of the many
large strawberry
black and red bulbs
of my body, were planets
that will serve as refuge
from this world
when it is gone. They see,
each of them, fully,
as a body, as my body,
as all bodies see

as a cockroach
as a horse
and as a snake

to be one
with the new weather

They still live in me.

The eclipse of the eternal
has entered the time
of my arrivals. No woman
nears the word
of entry or exit, she is ever present
within the eternal gun shot
score
of the absent. The young
earth, with its multitude
of arrangements of things,
calls to me
to reflect on the image
of a smile
that now has me
reach for the morning. Heat
erases the gains
of a stable mind, with exhaustion
and false silence, to which
I add the noise

of eternity.
The isthmus' Yoga
releases
her young body
the nameless one
of a thousand goats
from the names of witness. These goats
give me milk
to ease the crossings here. That
nourishment is Panamá. No
list can confuse the ejective
insistence of simplicity
with a lack of depth of others
here, in this country
expiring
because of the small view
on whom someone else depends
for a song. I call
the exceptionable Sun
to become a moment
of our seeing
the Kingfisher
fly beside us,
on the river. There is no
release from the slugs
of reduction, or from the sloths
from other worlds
that come to visit here

for us, through our instantaneous
video sorrows. Songs reform
the light outside, and grow
black roses, and stand
to mark the ground
for a mystery
that dissolves me.

And here

I dissolve again, as those things I engulf
to allow me to walk
in the world of those
who refuse to live
and will never
truly die
always entirely dead to you, North American
you who are
abandoned by the earth
as I was…

Death will absolve us again.

I breathe in the dark.

I breathe out the light.

Only sleep can attain the null erasure of the streets, of the bounded grasses
that make my arms fall for the bottom of sound. A traced intention, a calling
home filled with forests and mailing the exceptional ride of a chicken
to a forgotten departure, to the alerted eclipse that makes a reasonless line
fall to the actual silence of planted light, to the sentence that fills a shell
of her bus seduction, the momentary action plan that never realizes what will
attend to the forest, or to the fallen book of an absent limb, or to the unknown
as rain promises nests, the inference inscribed on neglect,
or gentle silence that was erased from home, or the abandoned number and room
of eternal wandering. A starving resilience, a tried amplitude that weakens the light
to see morning books and the connection there, to arrive at eerie reflectors
of pregnancy, this does not entertain the absolute segmentation and exceptional
future of a higher line. There is no sound or answer that relieves the limited view
from imagination, there is no origin to our intuitive riots that a calm resistance
does not reduce to a single and vast reply. No new poems are possible there. The asking
book will not start without the path that moves past each Eagle at fifty yards, as she
neutralizes the direction of the oar with her exploded heart. There is no attention equal
to the home that has erupted by this, there is not one sleepless aversion that the century will
remake to the full ascension of a single wing. This is an extinct language that no colorless
straw can ever know, and this is the mud that builds my simple shelter. The image and symbol of the seed
of all myth of bridges is created on this page, for the Yoga that will not stop at water, land, or animal. No
attention will ever reveal her witchcraft, the ship of a thousand lambs, to make flowers.

We are not just bags of chemicals, as you, the so called scientific claim
the electricity of her noise remains to undo an eclipse of the sound,
to visit again as the word remains to be brown, noiseless, and equivocal. One more coma
to fill the journey of refuge, the timeless structure of the gun, to return to the approaches
of plants that will not touch without secrets, these seeds will undo the silent gratitude that makes

one hear with a wordless soil. Two huge lockers full of guns

fill an attentive radio reception

to open a book without lines, the lookout that once turned memory to a touch

of flesh. Only a magnet can answer, as the maraca will cause the ascension of the white

growth in the snow, to snowball,

a multitude of eyes, the few hands, the desirous aggressions of the lonesome and peaceful

absence of words. I asked for the quiet of the storm, I asked for the plastic rod that makes refuge

return through the understanding of noise. I understand the other side of it, here, but do not map

the equivalent link to see one stand beside the market as one diminishes, with atrophies

and pursed receptions. They once sang that the eye of her regional light, the welcome face to see

one to be there with an edge, without bridges framing it,

and with a disk ejection

in the repetitive ice that will not decide or respond to the ideal operand,

the ideal absence of pathology, or no, the ideal pathologized mind that will not return

to this view, like the punctuation that eases the path through its own destructive

formlessness. The offensive refuge of the night, the return of light to roll back the informed

of this body, to enter the data and increase the circuit that makes the day start with a circumnavigating

ontology, to see there what still answer remains in the solitude of the entirely small. Lessons are burned

and the dungeon, the horseless lashes that move celebrity like the weatherman, the movie written

for the misspelled staring, the perfect encounter through the bus that makes chance dissolve the line

Poetry in a Time of War

for Rodrigo Toscano

Sometimes poetry becomes armor. It can be difficult to write poetry that is a form of vulnerability, not only vulnerability to others, but also to the universe. Anything can be made into armor: confession, the personal, politics, mythology, the everyday, views of nature, history, anything stylized and at rest or in motion, any angle. The same views can be used to allow us to be vulnerable, to be in motion and open, still and receptive. We can't stop at the merely personal, or at the merely formal to make a poetry without armor. The deciding line is the line which makes an approximate symmetry of our bodies. This line is the equator that writes the world in all directions.

I propose a poetry of vulnerability in a time of war, in any time where the word belongs. We must imagine evil, as a sound in the song of goodness, in this poetry. The devil face is a mask we can wear to celebrate it. Only a struggle with the demonic delivers a link to us all. This vulnerability is not only to the illusory outside, but from the illusion of us to the illusion of us. It implies a vibrational communion with others in how words and phrases break open, like seeds destroyed and created again in the coldness of space, then destroyed and created again in the volcanic origins of the earth. In this poetry the illusion of self and other dissolves, if we can see it, and we usually can't, but we can come closer and closer to that fact through its breathing. The vulnerable poet delivers hir words as they are spoken to us, as well from other times and other places, growing in the present as two hands put together. Not only the utility but the origin of the language that is being shared is under question. Did it appear as a miracle? Is muteness more true? Does it bind us to the world as water makes life possible? Its body becomes elemental and formless, able to mutate into any form and any spirit. It is the embodiment of silence. It is unity turned in on itself to be zero, resting there at the very beginning, unraveling in the light of the end.

The vulnerable allows us to experience the red and black sound, the sound born of islands in the tropics and from the geometries of snow in a crushing winter, both tied together by the Net. This sound is the blood of the black divine and the crisp cool night of collapse. It comes to us as the bridge between the senses. It erases the limits of the mouth and moves a pregnant soul through the earth. It is the underground home for the rabbit that writes for mystery, and for the snake that swallows the egg of the end of time.

Vulnerability is nonconceptual. It is timeless and fills space. Its sounds are always incomplete and strive for wholeness. It implies that every discomfort, every pain grows into a beaming sun, as the night sky is alive. Its satellites wander without aim. Its computation is a single table, Dual, which aims to be a bridge of the world. It is symbolic as each gesture is symbolic, and mythological as the only story ever told. It is psychic and psychotic, as it moves to end war with the mind, and makes love to everyone and everything eternally through a single body, without a notion of self. It is repulsed from things when the True and the False arrive and stand fast, an error of light. It overflows, as all signs arrive to bring us a new communion, the hole in time that allows us to be free.

The computer of vulnerability is the intermediate link between worlds. It is the ocean made plain and alive by the sky. It arrives as an egg in the palm of each poem, the circle of return to the plains without roads and the woods of our home. The computer is an ocean of toggles and as a bridge makes the weather arrive. It bleeds for the body of the world. It is the Start and the destiny of the word. It erases itself as poetry has erased itself, and allows us to make the first full circle, to belong to the earth as the weather changes to bring a first full meaning of our voice, through the sands and the organs of life, moved back and forth, and on and off, by the moon.

About Roberto Harrison

Roberto Harrison is the author of *Os* (subpress, 2006), *Counter Daemons* (Litmus Press, 2006), *bicycle* (Noemi Press, 2015), *culebra* (Green Lantern Press, 2016), *Yaviza* (Atelos, forthcoming 2017), as well as of many chapbooks. He is also a visual artist. He lives in Milwaukee with his wife Brenda Cárdenas.

Acknowledgments

Some of these poems first appeared in *Divine Magnet, Mandorla, Puerto del Sol, Palabra, Cream City Review, Aufgabe, The Cultural Society, Cannot Exist,* and *Th.ce*. A selection of these poems appeared as a chapbook entitled *Bridge of the World*, published by Cannot Exist. Many, many thanks to the editors.

green press
INITIATIVE

Litmus Press is committed to preserving ancient forests and natural resources. We elected to print this title on 30% post consumer recycled paper, processed chlorine free. As a result, for this printing, we have saved:

5 Trees (40' tall and 6-8" diameter)
2,236 Gallons of Wastewater
3 million BTU's of Total Energy
150 Pounds of Solid Waste
412 Pounds of Greenhouse Gases

Litmus Press made this paper choice because our printer, Thomson-Shore, Inc., is a member of Green Press Initiative, a nonprofit program dedicated to supporting authors, publishers, and suppliers in their efforts to reduce their use of fiber obtained from endangered forests.
For more information, visit www.greenpressinitiative.org.

Environmental impact estimates were made using the Environmental Defense Paper Calculator. For more information visit: www.papercalculator.org.